THE TWENTIETH CENTURY
HISTORIES OF FASHION

Series edited by
Ieri Attualità

THE TWENTIETH CENTURY
FASHION AND DRESS
Tentative titles

WOMAN

1. Evening dresses 1900 ... 1940 (Marco Tosa)
2. Evening dresses 1940 ... (Marco Tosa)
3. Maternity fashion (Doretta Davanzo Polí)
4. Skirts & more skirts (Flora Gandolfi)
5. Costume jewellery
6. Shoes for special occasions
7. Details: sleeves
8. Strictly personal: corsets and brassières
9. Petticoats & co.
10. Nightwear
11. Trousers for women
12. Day and evening bags
13. Blouses
14. Large and small hats
15. Hosiery and related items
16. Gloves
17. Cloaks and coats
18. Light coats and raincoats
19. Accessories for ladies: umbrellas and canes
20. Hairstyles
21. You can do anything with fur vol. 1
22. You can do anything with fur vol. 2
23. Casual shoes and boots
24. Afternoon and cocktail dresses
25. Shawls, scarfs and silk squares
26. Bridal gowns
27. Work-clothes
28. Beachwear and swimsuits
29. Details: necks and necklines
30. Belts and artificial flowers
31. Suits and daywear
32. Tricot and jersey fashions

CHILDREN

33. Children in their party dress (Nora Villa)
34. Girls
35. Children and brats
36. Children's shoes
37. Teenage boys
38. Teenage girls
39. Babies

MEN

40. Men's hats (Giuliano Folledore)
41. Furs for Men (Anna Municchi)
42. Trousers & co. (Vittoria de Buzzaccarini)
43. Work-clothes
44. Underwear
45. Shirts
46. Men's accessories: belts, gloves, ties and scarfs
47. Jackets
48. Waistcoats
49. Men's jewellery
50. Raincoats, ponchos and k-ways
51. Umbrellas, sticks and canes
52. Overcoats and coats
53. Pyjamas, robes etc.
54. Knitwear: cardigans and pullovers
55. Sportswear
56. Hairstyles, beards and mustaches
57. Shoes and boots
58. Uniforms
59. Suitcases, briefcases and bags
60. Swimsuits
61. Casualwear: blouson jackets and cabans

SPECIAL ITEMS

62. The handkerchief
63. Buttons
64. Ribbons round the world
65. Leather clothing
66. Jeans
67. T- and polo shirt
68. Glasses

FABRICS

69. Fabrics in fashions: cotton
70. Fabrics in fashions: wool
71. Fabrics in fashions: silk
72. Fabrics in fashions: man-made fabrics

FIORA GANDOLFI

Skirts and more Skirts

Zanfi Editori

ACKNOWLEDGEMENTS

The author would like to thank the following
people for their help:
Paloma Borrero de Gomez;
Enzo Bertoli;
Stefania Moronato of the Centro Studi di Storia
del Tessuto e del Costume, Palazzo Mocenigo,
Venezia;
Annie Segalow of the Musée de la Mode
et du Costume, Palais Galliera, Paris;
Giuseppe Pellissetti.

PHOTOGRAPHIC CREDITS

Photographs on pages 42, 44, 47, 48, 84, 85, 118
are from the Archive of the Centro Studi di Storia
del Tessuto e del Costume, Palazzo Mocenigo,
Venezia. Photographer Giacomelli.

The photograph on page 62 is from the
Raccolta Stampe Bertarelli, Milano.
Photographer Saporetti.

The drawings and the photograph on pages 104,
105 and 106 appear by kind permission of Enzo
Bertoli, Milano. Photographer Giacomelli.

All other illustrations are from the author's private
collection and the Ieri Attualità Archive.
Photographer Giacomelli.

Coordination: Vittoria de Buzzaccarini
Iconographic research: Ieri Attualità, Fiora Gandolfi
Editorial staff: Giuseppe Pellissetti, Elena Vezzalini
Graphic design: Giorgio Trani
Cover: Giorgio Trani and Studio Cancelli
Translation: Margaret Kearton - Logos Modena
Original title: Gonne e gonnelle

ISBN 88-85168-34-5

Il Novecento
Periodico - Aut. Trib. di Modena n. 904 del 18/01/88
N. 5 febbraio 1989 - sped. abb. post. GR. III/70
Publisher: Celestino Zanfi

INDEX

ORIGINES

THE CAVE-LADIES

The first woman known to us, Lucy, probably went about three million or so years ago with a striped or spotted animal fur tied around her waist by the legs.

At the end of the Old Stone Age, mankind invented weaving. The untreated woollen cloths they produced were tied round their chests or hips in just the same way as Lucy, the "Australopithecus" whose skeleton was discovered at Haddar, in Ethiopia, used to wear her furs.

Cave men and women both clothed themselves in the same type of garment: the skirt. And that's how it was for centuries.

The first documentation we have is provided by the sculptures of the Sumerians, between 2000 and 3000 B.C. There they are, with their eye make-up and their sumptuous apron-like goat-skin skirts, or "kaunakes", which tied at the back. These ancient inhabitants of Mesopotamia liked to have themselves portrayed in ceramic statues which were to remain in the temples for all eternity, and they always appear complete with bulky ankle-length skirts. The men and women taking part in ceremonies, or in the figurines on the altars of the gods, wear them without fail.

Unexpected new horizons were opened up to fur skirt technology thanks to the development of sharpened stones and combs. Parts of the furs were shaved, while other areas were combed, yet others "set" in waves, and the edges cut into zig-zags or fringes. Pelts were trimmed to represent leaves or birds.

7

1. The King of Mari *Iku Shamagan,* who lived in between 2000 and 3000 B.C., wore a *kaunakes* for prayer. The ritual fur skirt fastened at the back like an apron was sculpted with knives and scissors. National Museum, Damascus.

WRAP-AROUND SKIRTS IN BABEL

Long skirts gave women's (and above all men's) figures great authority, dignity and majesty. They remained the favourite form of dress of the Kings of Babylon.

The practical wrap-around skirt now made its first appearance in history. It was straight and made the figure slimmer, having a high-waisted shape with uneven turned-up edges. There was another novelty: it was held up by a draped diagonal shoulder strap. The kings of Babylon were barefoot, but the statue found at Akkad gives off an air of courteous authority, with the skirt (now made neither of fur nor of a cloth which imitated it) forming a kind of pedestal on which the head is enthroned. Loose pleats and light fabrics, so dear to the Indo-European peoples with whom the Babylonians were already in contact, came to the fore.

The Assyrians and Elamites, who dominated the Mesopotamian lands with differing fortunes, brought great innovations with them. Their light, flared skirts which reached down to cover their feet were densely decorated with tiny framing designs and printed patterns, or with straight or spiralling appliqué braids. For equestrian sports and for hunting, Assyrians wore little boots and decidedly shorter skirts giving more freedom of movement. They were cut on the bias at the front and featured a braid edging trim, while at the waist was a sash into which the ever-present, highly-treasured stiletto dagger was thrust.

DARIUS IN A 'PAREO'

In the 4th Century B.C. the artistic capital of the world shifted from Mesopotamia to Iran, thanks to the great Persian conquerors. Cyrus, Darius and Xerxes developed a cosmopolitan, modern image also influenced by the Phoenicians and Greeks. Fabrics became very lightweight and easy to drape. For official parades, Darius chose to exhibit himself at Persepolis sitting on a high throne and clad in a cool ankle-length skirt cut like a "pareo". However the skirt wasn't a royal privilege: even archers released their arrows dressed in patterned pareo skirts printed in shades of blue and gold.

The Egyptians were great designers, and must win the fashion prize for the ancient world. They introduced fringed wigs, eyes lengthened by cobalt and black make-up, and collars of turquoises and lapislazuli, or of coloured glass for the common people. In 1500 B.C. pleats made their appearance in Egypt. Women used them in long skirts, while the men had flared "minis". The primitive technique for the production of pleated fabric consisted of folding the cloth into the pattern required when wet, tying it at numerous points and placing the long strip obtained beneath hot stones to dry in the heat provided by the sun god Horus.

In Crete, dancing girls dressed in

2. This floor-length skirt, presumably in light fabric, alternates bands of pleats with embroidery and fringes. Queen Napir-Asu, the queen of Susa, has been wearing it in her bronze statue for more than 3000 years.

3.

3. The archer in Darius's palace at Sysab, immortalized in ceramics, wears a light ankle-length cotton skirt printed with stylized flowers using wooden dies. The edges of the fabric, which finish petal-fashion, are shown off by a frame with a continuous pattern.

4. In Egypt men's skirts were decorated with thin pleats and rich hanging belts, while skirts for women were tight-fitting showing the hips, with high waist and straps. Fresco in a tomb at Deyr el Medina near Thebes.

5. Another short skirt for men with shaped cut, worn wrap-over style, in light white linen gauze and fastened with a tie at the waist. A hunter of the New Empire. Fresco in the tomb of Nebamon near Thebes.

5.

sinuous flounced skirts which we would now describe as "folk" style. They were multi-coloured, flared into a bell shape, and divided into seven gathered flounces. A classical belt went round the waist, while a small apron was worn at the front. In this unusual ceremonial outfit priestesses bared their generously sized breasts in homage to the cult of the Great Mother.

From 2400 B.C. onwards Cretan women wore the most elegant skirts of the whole ancient world: these were flared, and decorated with braids and horizontal appliqués. They emphasized the curves of the figure below the fitted back, just as the skirts of Parisian women were to do in the Nineteenth Century. The Cretan design had a frill around the hem stiffened with jointed metal strips, which not only reinforced the bell-shaped silhouette but also jingled at every step. They were decorated with a Greek pattern, geometrical motifs or strange highly-coloured animals. Women had little freedom of movement, and the "sound-effects" allowed their jealous menfolk to keep tabs on them ... by music.

6. An Egyptian farmer of the Middle Empire ploughs his field wearing, like all the poor of the ancient world, a simple white skirt identical to the *pagnum* of the Roman slaves.

7. The Egyptian acrobatic dancer's minimal skirt is in printed cotton and ties simply at the front to show off the hips. New Empire. Museo Egizio, Turin.

8. The so-called "serpent goddess" of the palace of Knossos in Crete wears a skirt which opens out into seven multi-coloured gathered flounces beneath her full bare breasts and tight bodice. The outfit is completed by an apron with rounded edges.

7.

IMPERIAL TUNICS

In Athens and Rome people of standing always wore simple rectangles of cloth

6.

wrapped around their bodies in accordance with strict codes.

In fact, Greek and Roman garments were manifestations of the "draped style" which required no sewing of any kind and which had developed in the temperate regions on the European shores of the Mediterranean.

The peplum, which was just wrapped around the hips and can sometimes be seen in sculptures from the Greek and Roman civilizations, may be considered a kind of skirt, even if it was not intended as such.

The *himation*, on the other hand, was really a skirt. This garment reserved for kings and gods was often embroidered with flowers or lilies, or decorated with designs in gold or purple, or in a combination of the two. Phidias, the greatest sculptor of ancient Greece, represented Olympian Jove clad in a *himation*, in a colossal statue in ivory inlaid with gold.

Other ancient Greek skirts always appear in pictures of the Homerian heroes. Achilles, Hector, Patroclus and Diomedes all wore little skirts which just showed on their thighs beneath their splendid armour in precious metals decorated with magic engravings and protected by special divine benedictions: their function was to prevent the metal from chafing the skin.

Beneath his *lorica* Constantine, the first Christian Roman Emperor, dressed like the mythical warriors of the Iliad in a knee-length skirt consisting of wide strips of leather fringed at the hem. Then, with

11

8.

9. In Homeric times Greek and Trojan warriors allowed a very short skirt called the *chiton* to show beneath their armour.

10. The women and Queens of the barbarian Britons and Caledonians who inhabited Great Britain at the time of the Roman "occupation" wore skirts in woven fabric with horizontal stripes beneath their tunics.

10.

the passage of time and the evolution of clothing habits, the skirt, which had been the basic garment in the wardrobe of the ancients for centuries, disappeared from civilizations at all latitudes. It was replaced by the tunic, a loose-fitting garment of varying length and fullness, on whose empire the sun was not to set for at least eight centuries, until the late Middle Ages. It was to acquire and abandon various forms of decoration, indulging in embroidery and gold belts with a shower of precious stones or mortifying the wearer's as the harsh garment of the convent.

The tunic was adopted as their "prestige" garment by women of the barbarian peoples when they came into contact with the great Roman civilization. Their tall, bearded menfolk wore leather or woollen trousers, while barbarian ladies favoured huge skirts in heavy fabric which was sometimes figured and almost always striped, adding a more civilized touch by placing a brightly coloured silk tunic over the top.

FASHION'S CINDERELLA

In Italy during the Fifteenth and Sixteenth centuries the trade in, and production of, fabrics and elegant luxury items continued in spite of constant political upheavals. Even Pisanello turned designer to create sumptuous court costumes. Italian textiles attained unheard-of heights of luxury: taffetta, moire fabrics and "diaspro" brocade were all already available. No-one could match the Italians when it came to combining unusual materials and colours. The taste for luxury drove men and women to stud dresses, sleeves, hose and skirts with precious stones. Noble Italians and prelates alike all fell victims to the mania for perfection.

The skirt became the Cinderella of the clothing scene, worn only by peasant women, shepherdesses, laundresses, servants and cooks. It was in English or Dutch woollen cloth or in fustian (wool and cotton), featured an edging in other fabrics or in coloured braid, and was gathered at the waist where it was drawn in with a cord. A skirt in coarse, hand-woven cotton or hempen cloth, often dotted with patches, became the central item in traditional regional outfits from all over Italy. There are many illustrations showing the skirts of local costumes, all more or less in the same style: gathered at the waist and

11. In Jacopo Ceruti's painting a laundress wears a skirt gathered at the waist with a bodice and apron. This type of clothing for the lower classes dominated the scene without interruption for centuries, with the same style being worn by cooks, peasant women, and servants from Medieval times to the first decades of the Twentieth Century with small national or regional variations. Pinacoteca Tosio Martinengo, Brescia.

calf-length. Women nationwide had the sensible habit of covering this garment with an apron and with a chain hung with a few bits and pieces imitating the rich lady's jewels: a knife, a pair of scissors and a bunch of keys.

13

12. The highly-coloured skirts worn by ordinary women of all races were decorated with the thousand and one ideas which tradition and local craftsmen made available: embroidery, braids, ribbons, bows, buttons and filigree jewels. The style became fuller and fuller with gathers, folds and flounces. Skirts of different lengths were often worn one above the other for more volume. Hungarian traditional costumes of the 18th Century.

14

13.

14.

13. Swiss peasant women wore rather short skirts which just covered their knees, with a double edge trim. Gathered like all traditional skirts, they were worn with a little apron embroidered with little alpine flowers, while the legs were covered with heavy white cotton stockings.

14. Here the dialect is that of Brianza. The dress of this Lombard peasant woman at the end of the 19th Century is a timeless costume.

15. French female "citizens" at the end of the Eighteenth Century wore skirts in checked *toile Vichy* for working and also for dancing *rondes* around the liberty trees erected in the squares of towns and villages. Considerably shorter than those of the *Ancien Régime*, revolutionary skirts were in cotton printed with flowers or with patriotic red, white and blue stripes.

15.

"PANDORAS" AND PETTICOATS

From the Sixteenth Century onwards, in the absence of fashion magazines, mail-order catalogues or fashion parades, new styles were publicized using rag or wax dolls. The "grande Pandora" was used in Italy for formal outfits and the "piccola Pandora" for "negligées", or clothes for wear in the home. But even the dolls were never dressed in the skirt, in spite of the fact that this item of clothing was to become women's constant companion in our century.

Aristocratic ladies, followed a decade or so later by middle-class women, achieved truly astonishing effects in the lower halves of their figures.

The era of François I, a great admirer of Leonardo da Vinci, saw the introduction to France of the "farthingale", a petticoat in coarse, glue-coated hempen cloth with a hoop at the base which transformed women's bodies from the waist downwards into perfect cones. Not a fold was allowed in the skirts which made ladies into stiff cardboard puppets. The style had originated in Spain, where it was used to mask embarrassing pregnancies. In France it was known as the *vertugadin*, and the cone-shape became cylindrical.

Strangely enough, the menfolk also seemed to find the pompous appearance of these dresses seductive (perhaps they were attracted by the amount of rich fabric used, which created an air of power), and

16.

16. In the late 16th and early 17th Centuries skirts were ankle length for easy walking and were held out from the body by a rigid framework of metal, wicker or wood for less wealthy ladies. In France this went by the Spanish name of *vertugade*, which seems to have meant something like "virtue-guard". The Italian and French versions gradually became known as *garde-enfants*, which leads to suspect that rather than guarding the wearers' virtue the farthingale's main purpose was to cover up embarrassing slips.

17. Various examples of skirts from the 17th Century. At the time dresses were not yet sewn together, and the skirt and bodice of matching fabric which when worn together gave the impression of being all in one piece were in fact two separate items. These are the skirts of elegant French dresses. The white winter skirt in *moucheté* ermine with black tails was an extravagant luxury even for those times.

17.

a few years later they themselves took to wearing skirts of this type, in knee length over long hose: the change of sex was made clear by the new name given to this style, "Rhinegrave breeches". Men and women both seemed to be encased in strange barrels from the waist downward. The arms had to be held either stretched out or bent in a jug-like posture with hands on hips. During the Baroque age the fashionable French skirt became even more rich and pompous: the showy luxury of the fabrics imported from Venice was held in position by no less than three petticoats called the *secrète*, the *friponne* and the *modeste*.

SKIRTS ON CAGES

Imagination ran riot, and the centuries which followed witnessed a series of cages which gave completely unnatural shapes to the lower part of the female body, with the sole exception of the short interlude offered by the Empire Line.

20. Crinolines, or rather the fashion for skirts like hot air balloons. These very full skirts caught on all over Europe and at all levels in society. No duchess, housewife, shopkeeper or cook wanted to be without her swaying, fluttering skirt.

18. In the 18th Century the bulky size of the frivolously elegant skirt was reduced somewhat, especially for walks in parks and vegetable gardens during summer stays in the countryside. Giandomenico Tiepolo's fresco in the Villa Valmarana at Vicenza shows the folds of the ladies' skirts concentrated at the side over the hips. Delicate gilded braids decorate the full hems.

19. During the second half of the 18th Century skirts, complete with *paniers* became wider over the hips and were decorated with laces, bows and frills. For the summer they were in linen with lingerie style embroidery or in light cotton fabrics printed with stripes or flowers which came from England, where the cotton industry had undergone considerable development after 1750. Middle-class fashions required more streamlines skirts which still allowed for a certain coquettishness.

19.

17

20.

The panier, double panier and *Thérèse* (a cumbersome series of wicker hoops whose bulk also aimed it the nickname of *calèche* or *carriage*) followed one another in dizzying sequence. The wicker or metal cage soon came back into fashion, but this time it was fitted with hinges to allow it to be folded up under the arm while its wearer performed the tricky operation of climbing into a carriage. Then the panier, typical wear of Eighteenth Century ladies, seemed to have been abolished for ever by the French Revolution.

But this was not the case. To support the wide flares of Nineteenth Century skirts or "crinolines", composed of frills and soft frothy laces, bamboo or metal cages were once again a necessity. This time, they were produced by a metal-working company of Mulhausen in Alsace called Peugeot, who at that time manufactured not motor cars but iron petticoats and made a mint of money.

Later, when crinolines, which had reached such inordinate dimensions that they had even been known as "balloons", finally went out of fashion a hundred or so years ago, the curves of the female figure were enhanced by the so-called *cul de Paris*, or bustle, a half-moon shaped pad worn over the behind and fastened round the waist with a ribbon tied at the front. It was first favoured by the aristocracy and caught on with the middle classes after about ten years.

21.22.23. Whether paying a visit or travelling, out for a stroll, at the theatre or dancing, the romantic lady of the Nineteenth Century was always hampered by her crinoline. But the iron will of fashion decreed that without one of these huge skirts, which could measure up to 18 metres in circumference at the hem, a woman was no longer *à la page*.

MODES VRAIES.
Travail en famille

MUSÉE DES FAMILLES

19

SKIRTS AND DEMOCRACY

But by the end of the Nineteenth Century fashions were taking on a more democratic air. The metabolic rate of the fashion world was speeding up. An Englishman named Worth invented a feminine version of the classical masculine ensemble of shirt, jacket and trousers, which were transformed into skirts for the occasion.

Since ladies did not spend paying and receiving calls, a skirt and blouse were adopted as everyday wear in the home. Giving orders to the servants, embroidery, piano lessons, reading and decorative painting were the main features of the home lives of elegant middle-class ladies who dressed in green, grey, blue, dove-coloured or mole-grey skirts combined with embroidered silk or cotton blouses trimmed with jabots and lace frills. These were "working" clothes, and immediately became the basic if not the only uniform of schoolteachers, students and governesses,

24.

24. Irish lace skirts which alternated openwork embroidery with braid, beading and eyelet lace.

25. Examples of the practical, elegant skirts available in 1900. The first is in black silk taffetta with a hint of a train and a flounce of ruffles, while the others, with flat pleats and flounced motif were intended for wear in the home. *La Saison* 1910.

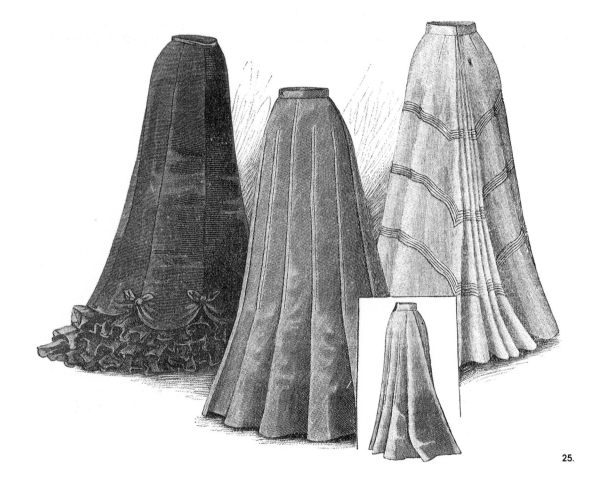

25.

20

26. A "dirt-resistant" woollen fabric for the "busy" woman's skirt at the end of the 19th Century.

who favoured anonymous grey fabrics which had the virtue of "not showing the dirt". Madame Curie was also wearing a skirt and blouse in 1898 when, in the dark storeroom rigged up as a laboratory in her Paris home, she discovered radium: "spontaneously luminous phosphorescent, bluish particles which have something more attractive than just a beautiful colour."

SKIRTS FOR MEN

As we have already seen, in ancient times men also wore skirts with dignity as well as women. Even though nowadays their use is limited to Greece and Scotland, skirts for men are still definitely martial garments.

The Greek *euzones* wear short skirts with tight pleats at official ceremonies and when they mount guard at the tomb of the unknown soldier in Syntagma Square in Athens. These are combined with white tights and large black wool pompoms.

This original military uniform, which has survived down the centuries, derives from Balkan costumes of Turkish inspiration, still found in the folk traditions of Herzegovina and Albania, where knee-length white skirts are worn with embroidered boleros. The Scottish kilt is of Celtic origin. During the Sixteenth Century Nicolay de Arfeville, the King of France's astronomer

27. The *Euzones,* the Greek soldiers who wear the characteristic uniform with the little pleated mini skirt in woven cloth.

visited Scotland and provided a description of the inhabitants who "wore a skirt coloured with saffron, and over this a heavier woollen garment reaching down to the knee."

The immediate predecessor of the kilt itself, called the "breacan-féile" or "féile-beag" appeared towards the Seventeenth Century. A cloth edging came away from the lower pleated section to the shoulder, where it was fastened with a brooch.

Nowadays the kilt is a tightly pleated skirt with a pleatless fringed front, worn with a tweed jacket with horn buttons. It is decorated with the famous sporran, a purse made from leather and marten or fox fur. The kilt (beneath which no intimate apparel must be worn) is never held up with braces and must reach down to the hollow at the back of the knee. The best way of getting the right length is to try on your kilt when kneeling down: it should just brush the floor. Four and a half yards of tartan fabric are needed to make a kilt. The patterns each belong to one of the 96 clans, and it is clear that a member of the Keer family (red/brown and green) will never be seen in a MacArthur (green/blue with yellow line).

21

27.

28.29. The soldier and the Liberal who weeps over the grave of his party and the whisky which comforts his countryman from a poster are both pure bred Scots with kilt and sporran.

30. Faithful to tradition, the members of the British royal family wear kilts when they stay at Balmoral in the heart of Scotland. The Prince Consort, who has no Scottish blood in his veins, prefers a pair of trousers. Photograph Patrick Lichfied, 1972.

THE NEW STYLES

SKIRTS AND SUFFRAGETTES

At the beginning of the new century, the female silhouette when seen in profile was a snakey "S" shape. Two exaggerated curves emphasized the line of the bottom and bust, and breathing was very difficult. Anyone who placed the palm of their hand on a lacy bosom would have felt the beating of a heart racing like that of a frightened bird, imprisoned in the sharp stays of a whalebone corset. And yet feminism had already been born. In London the "poor little match-girls" had won a small social battle. The women workers in the cigar factories in Venice had fought against the gendarmes in city's squares for a reduction in their working hours. The dedicated English suffragettes, who came from an intellectual élite, had held noisy processions through central London streets. But none of them had said a definite "No" to the corsets which "hygienically moulded" the body, dividing it into halves whose curves were more or less pronounced depending on social class. Underneath their large shawls, the cigar makers of the Venetian lagoon wore tight bodices and big skirts in coloured cloth with gathered flounces, with their traditional flat slippers on their feet.

Women of the enlightened middle classes were unable to free themselves

31. Black and green woollen fabric with tartan pattern cut on the cross for this skirt with round pleats stitched flat at the front and left open at the back to accentuate the hourglass figure. The belt fastens at the back in "double-breasted" style with eight buttons. *La Mode Pratique* 1906.

24

32.

from the dictates of respectability, and they wore skirts which fitted tightly on the hips, with tightly laced corsets.

They followed social and cultural developments while wearing the most elaborate hairstyles, and were not averse to immense hats like feathery galleons. Of course, a woman could not attend a university wearing a lace and chiffon skirt in "peach Melba" colour as suggested by fashion magazines in 1901 without meeting with

32. Also for spring 1906 another suggestion from *La Mode Pratique* is this very elegant skirt in lightweight striped wool in grey and beige. The original Greek-type stitched patterns are created with stripes of fabric cut to shape: the centre is in red velvet.

33. For spring 1906 the waistline of the skirt was shifted decidedly upwards towards the bust, which was supported by bones sewn on the inside. The bodice-skirt trimmed with stitching near the hemline and the typical flat panel at the front is in mélange cloth. Two-piece suit with Milan-style buttons and braid trim. *La Mode Pratique* 1906.

33.

disapproval. Laces and sweeping skirts were of course also ruled out by common sense for the few women who worked in offices, or (horror of horrors!) in factories.

Only children and teenagers wore calf-length skirts, often with a frill it was practically their uniform. On their feet they wore high boots tightly buttoned using a special little hooking device. A lot of famous voices were raised against "trailing" skirts.

On 2nd March 1902, the Italian magazine *Domenica del Corriere* published the very popular column "In casa e fuori" (Inside and Outside the Home). A note for ladies informed readers that "determined couturiers in Germany and England have set themselves the task of reforming female clothing from head to toe, freeing it from the tyranny of the corset and from the risk of spreading the germs of countless diseases by transporting them in exaggeratedly long skirts".

The drawing with unattractive silhouette suggested by the "Healthy and Artists Dress Union" left the legs clearly in view from the knees downward, even if they were modestly clad in black cloth gaiters. The idea was a strange caricature, and met with no success.

"It is true that the outfit is practical, and useful in a lot of ways, but it is highly unattractive, or even almost ridiculous", commented our unknown journalist.

And so in the name of femininity women workers continued to spend dangerous hours in workshops full of machinery "with the risk of sustaining injury if a fold of their clothing catches in the gears".

Professional women in both England and America, the first women graduates in medicine or law, and pianoforte or art students all lived in peril of tripping up as they got on or off their omnibuses, since at every move they had to remember their long skirts, which were only a little shorter than those worn in the drawing room.

34. This drawing shows almost all the fashion possibilities as far as skirts were concerned for spring 1906. The folds could be large, small, sewn down, box-type, loose or like those in nuns' habits. Decorative motifs included flounces, frills, insets of different fabrics, shaped appliqués, braid and *soutaches* which formed embossed designs. There were also stitching, guipure beading and buttons. All these skirts shared the line, inevitably tilted forwards, required by the 1906 fashion for the hourglass figure.
La Mode Pratique 1906.

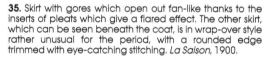

35. Skirt with gores which open out fan-like thanks to the inserts of pleats which give a flared effect. The other skirt, which can be seen beneath the coat, is in wrap-over style rather unusual for the period, with a rounded edge trimmed with eye-catching stitching. *La Saison*, 1900.

36. Visiting or walking outfit with flat pleats and train, featuring a double skirt effect provided by the velvet braid. *La Saison* 1900.

37. At the beginning of the 20th Century the American designer Charles Dana Gibson invented the new prototype of the working girl for *Life* magazine. She wore a provocative outfit consisting of a flared grey skirt, white blouse, black necktie and small hat.

Oddly enough, the train, which had already been in fashion for some time, tended to become longer during the opening years of the Twentieth Century. In walking or house dresses it was only very slight, but for formal evening occasions it became a stately tail. It is interesting to note that the officially fashionable skirt, as described in luxury fashion magazines during the first three years of the Twentieth Century (a period full of social tension) became decidedly less practical and longer in length even at the front, where it posed a considerable threat to life and limb. Hemlines became absurdly, dangerous long: skirts had to have 4, 5 or even 8 cm of fabric resting on the floor. Although the great fashion creators of the age were

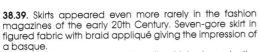

38.

39.

40.

27

38.39. Skirts appeared even more rarely in the fashion magazines of the early 20th Century. Seven-gore skirt in figured fabric with braid appliqué giving the impression of a basque.
Elegant summer skirt in tartan silk which draws in the abundant fulness at the back to provide the hourglass line required in the early years of the century. The double flounce trimmed with ribbon repeats the ever-present idea of the upturned vase. *La mode illustrée*, 1903.

40. Never separated from the petticoats which corrected their hang by holding out their hemlines, skirts were generally used by teachers and governesses who adopted a model in rustling black taffeta with an attractive play on ribbing and loose pleats for more formal occasions connected with their work. *La mode illustrée*, 1906.

concentrating their attention on the dress, (even though this was often actually in three pieces: top, skirt and belt) individual skirts were also available on their own. They were offered as a sporting, practical, no-nonsense alternative rather as jeans are nowadays.

The guiding spirits behind a crusade in favour of more practical clothing for women were Bernard Shaw, Oscar Wilde and the American fashion designer Charles Gibson, who offered an outift consisting of a skirt and blouse combination.

The famous Gibson Girl had a fresh, dynamic image. This provocative style of dress, immediately accepted and appreciated by working women even at the end of the Nineteenth Century, was worn by fashionable

41. A skirt's elegance also depended on the quality of the petticoat with which it was worn, to which the large stores gave a great deal of importance. During the first decade of the 19th Century petticoats were generally in percalle, only occasionally in silk or flannel for winter. They were close-fitting, and gored to flare out at the hemline like flowers, with gathered frills with lots of cotton lace, ribbons, braid and *entredeux*. In delicate colours such as white, mauve, sky blue, pink and cream if in cotton, they became more aggressive and coquettish in black, purple or red in silk versions. They measured 80 - 105 cm at the back to emphasize the train.

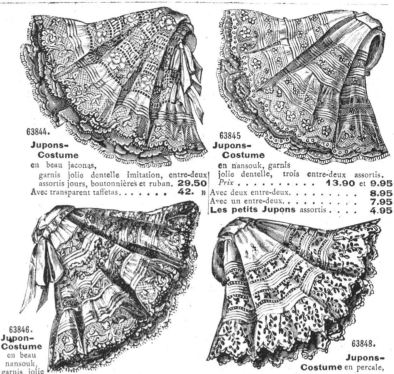

63844.
Jupons-Costume
en beau jaconas, garnis jolie dentelle imitation, entre-deux assortis jours, boutonnières et ruban. **29.50**
Avec transparent taffetas . . . . . . **42. »**

63845
Jupons-Costume
en nansouk, garnis jolie dentelle, trois entre-deux assortis.
Prix . . . . **13.90** et **9.95**
Avec deux entre-deux. **8.95**
Avec un entre-deux. **7.95**
Les petits Jupons assortis **4.95**

63846.
Jupon-Costume
en beau nansouk, garnis jolie dentelle imitation, entre-deux assortis, jours et ruban . . . **18.75**
63847. Avec deux entre-deux **14.90**

63848.
Jupons-Costume en percale, garnis belle broderie anglaise, entre-deux et plis. 7.95, 9.95 et **12.90**
Avec un entre-deux. 6.50 et 7.90 | **Les petits Jupons.** 3.95 et **4.90**

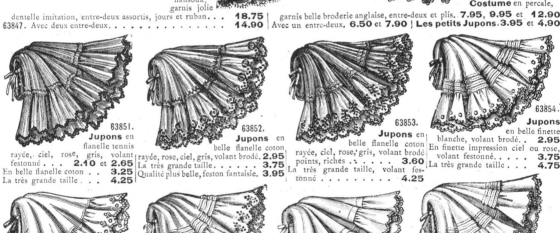

63851.
Jupons en flanelle tennis rayée, ciel, rose, gris, volant festonné . . . **2.10** et **2.65**
En belle flanelle coton . . **3.25**
La très grande taille . . **4.25**

63852.
Jupons en belle flanelle coton rayée, rose, ciel, gris, volant brodé. **2.95**
La très grande taille. **3.75**
Qualité plus belle, feston fantaisie. **3.95**

63853.
Jupons en belle flanelle coton rayée, ciel, rose, gris, volant brodé points, riches **3.60**
La très grande taille, volant festonné **4.25**

63854.
Jupons en belle finette blanche, volant brodé. . **2.95**
En finette impression ciel ou rose, volant festonné. **3.75**
La très grande taille . . . **4.75**

63855.
Jupons en finette, volant brodé. **3.25**
En belle flanelle crème, ciel, rose, mauve, rouge, volant feston fantaisie et pois. **5.50**

63856.
Jupons en belle finette blanche, volant brodé et plis. **3.25**
Qualité plus belle, volant festonné.
Prix **3.95**

63857.
Jupons en belle finette blanche, feston main. **3.25** et **3.95**
La très grande taille **4.50**
En piqué molletonné. **4.95** et **5.90**
La très grande taille **6.50**

63858.
Jupons en finette blanche, belle qualité, feston main et plis.
Prix . . . . . . **3.95** et **4.50**
La très grande taille. . . . **4.95**
En très belle flanelle crème, rose, mauve, rouge. **7.50** et **8.90**

63859.
Jupons en belle finette blanche, volant brodé main . . . **4.50**
Pantalons assortis. . . **3.60**

63860.
Jupons en belle flanelle crème, ciel, rose, mauve, rouge, volant brodé coton mercerisé . . **4.95**
Plus riche, brodé soie. . . **6.90**

63861.
Jupons en belle flanelle crème, ciel, rose, mauve, rouge, volant broderie anglaise. **6.95**
En crépon de laine. . . **8.90**

63862.
Jupons en belle flanelle crème, ciel, rose, mauve, rouge, volant brodé, entre-deux assorti **9.90**
Sans entre-deux **7.95**

28

42-46. Elegant skirt with loose folds in black taffeta for wear with a macramé jacket. *Regina* 1905. The high waist of the skirt of the elegant visiting ensemble reached to just below the bust and was attached to the patterned *chemisette* by press-studs. The slight train is decorated with a play on interwoven bands of fabric enlivened with mother of pearl buttons. The skirt in the next *toilette de promenade* fits above the cloth petticoat which supports the two flounces cut on the cross, trimmed with a double edging of braid. The original three-flounce motif which is repeated on the bodice of the jacket and at the bottom of the flared sleeves offers all the Liberty style's favourite elements. The blue cloth skirt worn with the sumptuous chinchilla winter jacket is trimmed with fur on the hem. Two additional bands of fur conceal the seam attaching the large flounce cut on the cross, which was present at the hemline of all the outfits of this era. The skirt of the final outfit is made up of flared pleats which provide a flounced effect at the hem in chiné grey wool. The seams which close the pleats are trimmed with sky blue wool brade 3 cm wide. The *chemisette*, which matches the suit perfectly, is in light sky blue silk crepe pleated throughout. *La mode illustrée*, 1901; 1902; 1903.

ladies only on informal occasions at home, on picnics or during those thrilling bicycle outings offering such healthy fresh air.

Skirts were invariably worn by strict governesses or by ladies busy embroidering cupids or roses in drawn-work under the magnolia in the garden. They were held out by forthy *jupons* in light cotton or warm flannel, always trimmed with lace. The dark colour of the skirt itself contrasted with the filmy brightness of the white lace blouse with its high collar supported by boning. The whole outfit seemed to be designed as a continual reminder of woman's

46.

fragility: she was unable to stand up straight without the aid of whalebone.

The numerous, but expensive, fashion magazines made little mention of the skirt as distinct from the dress. When it did appear, for winter, spring and autumn wear, it was in a masculine fabric, and was often accompanied by a short bolero and a very elaborate white blouse.

Tailored suits were fairly widely recommended for shopping expeditions to the town's most elegant establishments. The skirts were gored or opened out into fans of pleats carefully pressed with a heavy flat-iron. To get round the hygiene - or rather pavement-sweeping - problem, a strip of furry fabric was applied to the inside edge of the hem. This acted as a kind of brush and was changed as soon as it became worn.

ART NOUVEAU STYLE

The Liberty, Art Nouveau, "Novecento" or *Jugendstil* movement, to list a few of its names, drew fashions into its sphere of influence, creating a fashion for skirts which hung sinuously around the legs in voluptuously flowing, rustling fabrics.

During the golden age of Klimt's art, a woman's walk had to be like the supple unwindings of a tropical plant. The common skirt had to resemble a lithe, graceful flower: the campanula.

Diagonal flounces in velvet, satin or the same fabric, appliqué braids, silk cords

49. An outfit consisting of skirt and jacket in embroidered linen, for summer wear. In 1907 skirts were so long that walking in the open air became a problem. *Les Modes* 1907.

30

47. A frothy, 18th Century style skirt for the beach, in chantilly and organza with love-knots, flowers and rosettes in silk and lace. High fashion did not allow clothes to be changed depending on the time of day: fragile fabrics and laces were used even at the seaside. *Les Modes* 1907.

48. The skirt of this elegant travelling suit is perhaps rather too long to make getting on and off the train very easy. In checked alpaca, with tucks and decorated at the hem with solid colour taffetta. *La mode illustrée*, 1904.

47.

48.

in Cechov's *Three Sisters*, who teaches in a grammar school, wears the long, cumbersome grisaille skirts required by convention, even though she feels in the atmosphere that "a violent, healthy storm" is on its way.

TAILORED SUITS AND SKIRTS FOR SPORT

The tailored suits or *tailleurs* worn by ladies who had to spend their days outside the drawing-room revealed a justified distaste for lace and frivolity. These suits were a literal transcription of those worn by men. They were also a logical reaction to the aesthetic excesses which reached their greatest heights at this point in the century just as all forms of hand crafting, such as cabinet-making, glass working, wrought iron working and the rest, also attained their highest levels of perfection during this period.

Fashionable designers insisted that the female image had to be frilly, soft and lingerie-like, but fashion creators of a more progressive bent worked on producing outfits more appropriate to the practical realities of everyday life.

English magazines expressed the new progressive ideology, first cautiously and then with conviction, connecting the middle class way of life with the comfort of adaptability. As everyone knows, the English love the countryside and they were the first in the world to grasp the importance of changing dress for different times of day. For morning wear, for country walks, they designed a series of skirts in fabrics and colours which were not too delicate. The first sports skirts were born. Trains

51. On the beach for a picnic, when the Venice Lido was only a strip of sand, ladies wore full skirts trimmed at the hemlines with a wide frill 7 cm wide, below which the lace of their petticoats could be seen. Skirts for beachwear in 1900 were white for younger ladies and black for those who were a little older.

33

had disappeared and ankles were now visible. Sports skirts were worn by cyclists, tennis-players and the courageous Italian women climbers immortalized in an illustration by Beltrame in the *La Domenica del Corriere* (31st July, 1904). They were flared grisaille skirts of mid-calf length, worn with woollen stockings, nailed shoes and khaki-coloured woollen blouses with a Russian-style side fastening.

The skirts worn for enjoyable games of tennis were always white and did not abandon lace altogether, while the cycling styles were in mélange colours.

For springtime strolls across meadows full of wild flowers, or for expeditions to admire the progress of the new airships and breathe a little fresh air, the preference was for cotton skirts with a light check.

As we have seen, the English tried to

52. The intrepid skier Mademoiselle Lacroix exhibited her skills on the snow in daring descents with skis close together. Her skirt for the occasion was casual, slightly flared and mid calf length. *Femina* 1909.

53. The young lady at the Deauville races in the impressive hat with the feathers and holding the parasol is wearing a soft silk tunic, and a skirt with two overlapping flounces decorated with pleats and little folds. *Les Modes* 1907.

54. The ladies' riding outfit was produced by a specialist tailor, who generally produced mainly suits for men. The style was unchanging: it was a special long, very full skirt with an abundant wrap-over and side fastening. *Femina* 1909.

52.

53.

54.

55.

55. Aviation and skirts are incompatible: all honour and modesty would be lost if a providential loop, probably of string, didn't solve the problem. *Femina* 1909.

56. Mademoiselle De Bellet, the newly crowned French golf champion, wears a gored skirt with pockets over her gaiters with great style. *Femina* 1912.

57. Tennis clothes were always white and the skirt was full, comfortable and ankle length. Mademoiselle Boquedis poses authoritatively after a satisfying victory. Her very long white skirt hangs in loose folds beneath a cardigan with a broad white trim. *Femina* 1912.

56.

57.

reconcile the middle-class lifestyle with more practical considerations. The French, who were much more devoted to life in town, continued to offer elegance at an international level, especially filmy lightweight dresses. In autumn it was quite common to see princesses mud-splattered to the knee because they had not yet thought of selecting and organizing their wardrobes in relation to the time and the season. Perhaps they were so used to going about by carriage that they did not know that streets could also be muddy. During the early years of the century, any woman whose finances and lifestyle permitted, queens, princesses or theatre or opera stars dressed in the morning as though preparing for a "soirée."

FABRICS AND COLOURS OF THE EARLY TWENTIETH CENTURY

In the opening years of the century skirt fabrics were woollen serge or cloth with a stiff, full handle.

During the coldest months of the year

58. Blue or grey serge or woollen cloth were the ideal fabrics for cycling skirts. Pedalling diligently along the avenues in shady parks, country roads or along the shores of a lake was the new sport permitted to girls and young ladies in the Twentieth Century. *La mode illustrée* 1900.

59. Yachtswomen wore long tartan skirts with loose pleats drawn in at the waist by a sailor-style belt for their battles with wind and sails. *Femina* 1909.

the colours were dull and metropolitan: asphalt or cement grey, various shades of bronze and a very dark bottle green. The contrasting fabrics used to decorate the flounce varied from velvet to moire, and even gathered crêpe de chine was used.

Skirts increasingly tended to feature horizontal, parallel pleats decorating the area directly above the hem, and braid used to form attractive button-holes for "Milan-style" buttons. The silhouettes which caught the eye on the street during elegant strolls were haughty and sober. Colours were strictly tone-on-tone, from the flowery, feathery hat to the muff, the long stole in skunk or another long-pile,

60.

61. For morning walks in early autumn the fashion was for delicate neutral colours ranging from khaki and mushroom to rosewood. The skirts visible beneath the jackets had shortened to reveal the shoes. The basically severe line was enlivened a little by very flat pleats and a braid trim which forms a dense looped fastening and groups of pleats which form panels held in place at the sides by a play on button holes and small buttons. *Femina* 1909.

60. At the beginning of the Twentieth Century ladies climbed mountains in skirts, and Italian climbers wore very warm wool skirts with felt hats and boots suitable for the conditions. *La Domenica del Corriere* 1904.

37

61.

62.

62. The girl students who attended high schools and universities and boarding school girls were dressed practically all alike in skirts with large pleats short enough to allow them to walk comfortably in their high-buttoned boots of shiny black leather.

63. The skirt and blouse were homewear par excellence. This is a "princely" informal skirt worn by Elizabeth, the wife of Albert, heir to the Belgian throne, who is giving a music lesson to her little son Leopold. *Femina* 1909.

dark-coloured fur, and the skirt itself.

For the spring a little more imagination came into play, but dark shades were still *de rigueur* for the light wool fabrics with very large or very small tartan checks, which tended to be in woodland colours. Also given free rein were dry-handle English wool cloths in natural tones from grey to greyish beige which contrasted with the pure white of the blouse. The buttons and "Milan-style" button-holes in red silk cord which stood out on the navy blue serge skirts gave a slightly minxish touch.

For the warmest months, attractive skirts in écru cotton muslin also appeared. They played on the transparent effects provided by lace and guipure beading, or were made lighter in appearance by areas of pleats distributed garland-like just above the hem. Another important feature were the very long rows of buttons carefully positioned in the centre front, as in the many examples displayed in the large stores' mail-order catalogues.

63.

THE END OF THE "BELLE EPOQUE"

OLYMPIC SKIRTS

As on previous occasions, it was the English who suggested the next round of changes and revolutions in the world of the skirt, at the beginning of the second decade of the century. This time it was all due to their irrepressible passion for sport, heightened by the fourth Olympic Games held in London in 1908. These Games were to have been held in Imperial Rome, against the setting of the Forum which had just been unearthed.

But bickering between the Northern and Southern Italians led to hesitations and the event moved from the unreliable banks of the Tiber to the more reassuring site beside the Thames. The craze for sport and exercise infected the whole population of Great Britain. De Coubertin's statement that "the important thing is not to win, but to take part" was taken literally by the inhabitants of Albion. 1910 saw the birth of countless private sports clubs, the most progressive of which accepted the gentle sex amongst their exclusive membership. Golf, tennis, running and jumping led to scissors being taken to the hemlines of skirts. The feet came into view, and cries of

64. This shooting outfit in checked wool has a daringly short skirt which shows the legs clad in very high gaiters. The skirt is unfastened to allow easier walking, showing a whole colour underskirt. The stitching on the hemline and side emphasize the effect of the three button holes.
Journal des dames et des modes 1912.

horror were heard from moralists convinced that shoes on display signified corruption and the end of the civilized world. These apocalyptic forecasts seemed to be reinforced by the innocent approach of Halley's comet, which was speeding its way across the skies of Europe just on cue, in June 1910. This elegant heavenly body brought in its train rumours that divine punishment would be distributed through its luminous tail which, as rumour had it, was rich in "cyanogen" gas. Luckily, the forecasts that legions of sporting women would be asphyxiated had no foundation in reality.

65.

66.

65. An original skirt for a suit in black Cheviot wool with the trimming providing the effect of a double skirt in black and white checks. *Femina* 1912.

66. The mole-grey suit in Cheviot wool cloth follows the new fashion trends faithfully: tight-fitting skirt, with unsymmetrical features and decorated with "brandebourgs", buttonholes whose large size gave them a military air. *La mode pratique* 1911.

The skirt, whose history in many ways runs parallel to that of the emancipation of women, made gradual progress thanks to a succession of underground battles won in the wardrobe of time, supplanting the severe, boring, immensely less convenient dress. During relaxing, cheerful rides out on the tandem, thrilling spins in the motor car or hard-fought tennis matches, women dealt lasting blows against the column-like skirts which made them feel solemn and important, but trapped in history.

Floor-sweeping hemlines gradually disappeared from the fashion scene not only for sporting occasions but also in every-day life. Shoes with buckles and heels were clearly in view, and going for walks was much less complicated.

67.68. The draped effects in skirts from the 1910s recall Nineteenth-Century puffs or give the *jupe-culotte* a more civilized look. *Femina* 1914.

69. Casual, very modern identification of this model with Flora. She wears a long, draped *jupe-culotte* in heavy white crepe de chine. *Journal des dames et des modes* 1913.

42

TROUSER SKIRTS FOR THE FEMME FATALE

The need to get rid of trains, floor-length skirts and frills and furbelows had been felt at all levels in society. The respected voices of writers, doctors and artists were raised in harmony with the discontented mutterings of women themselves.

But couturiers continued to create as if nothing had changed.

In 1910 there was a clear dichotomy between the fixed, clearly established but spiritually *démodé* image of the skirt as it had been previously and the dictates of common sense. The activities of workers' movements throughout Europe inspired fear in the hearts of governments, and of the Pope, who preached calm and immobility.

In 1911 a news story shocked the world: unknown hands stole, or rather kidnapped, that unscrutable, unchanging symbol of eternal femininity, Leonardo da Vinci's *Monna Lisa*, from the Louvre Museum in Paris. It was a symbolic event. In the same year the "scandalous, vulgar and absurd" trouser skirt appeared to deal another blow to the mystique of femininity. It immediately became highly controversial.

Yet its appearance wasn't in the least provocative. It was the concept of trousers for women which created all the unease. In reality, the garments created were clumsy bell-shaped skirts with lots of loose folds, separated between the legs by a well hidden central division. But this was enough to cause all the uproar. The very name wreaked chaos wherever it was mentioned.

In the meantime a *jupe culotte* of clearly oriental inspiration with sumptuous choice of fabrics and decorations was designed by Paul Poiret, the high society French couturier, who was the first of his ilk to interest himself in skirts. All the ladies of the elegant élite were seduced and transformed into members of the harem by the unusual outfits which they wore on every brilliant society occasion. This luxury version of the divided skirt was also the object of a real witch-hunt all over Europe, even in Russia. The director of a St. Petersburg theatre was forced to place the following notice in the lobby: "I find myself obliged to forbid the entrance of women in trouser skirts. This does not mean that I personally disapprove of the above garments. However, as is well known, they give rise to sensations and comments which could jeopardize the quiet needed in a theatre. And since I cannot allow a second theatre to start up inside our theatre here, I find myself forced to take this decision."

...AND HOBBLED ANKLES

The real fashion revolution in this part of the century was the disappearance of the corset. Skirts, like all other items of clothing, were visibly affected by this change: the waistline was no longer drawn in by whalebone, and skirts hung with a more flowing line. Paul Poiret, the great fashion innovator of the period, reinter-

70.

70. "Lemons", a *jupe-culotte* for summer wear designed by Lepape for a Paul Poiret creation. *La Gazette du Bon Ton*, 1913.

71. Four ways of "culotte-ing" women. An explanatory drawing by Paul Poiret. *Illustration* 1911.

71.

preted themes from Europe's past and then cast his gaze eastward to China and Russia.

But ladies, who had finally been freed from their corsets, were able to allow themselves only a short sigh of relief. The tyranny of fashion decided that they were not to be left in liberty to rush headlong towards the future and progress. The comportment, behaviour and stately grace required of the elegant lady remained unchanged. Poiret made innovations, but he had no intention of creating the image of a young, sporting, dynamic woman. Between 1910 and 1913 the idea of beauty was a mixture of mature authority and a slightly exotic eclecticism. Finally, women were able to breathe properly, but alas, they were now prevented from walking. A strip of fabric known as the *entrave* or, more graphically, the "hobble", drew in the skirt and restricted all movements at ankle height, forcing the wearer to take short steps in the manner of a Chinese lady with bound feet. The hobble, which created almost a bobbin-shape effect, was applied

44

73.

72. The skirt of this elegant outfit is in silk muslin. The slightly draped *entrave* of the same fabric is fastened by a bow. *Journal des dames et des modes* 1913.

73. The *entrave* or hobble caught in the full skirt below the knee. Designed to hold the skirt in place in case of unexpected gusts of wind, it immediately caught on and slowed down walking considerably. *Margherita* 1912.

to high-waisted, rather shapeless skirts full on the hips, with few decorations, braidings, ribbons or pleats.

The story went that this fashion had been designed for the sporting, high-society or curious females who had been attracted to the primitive airfields where the first experimental flights were taking place. The breeze created by the propellers lifted the skirts of the onlookers in a most improper way. Poiret was scandalised and solved the problem by inventing the hobble.

CHANGES IN SKIRTS

1912 - 1916 saw a series of rapid changes which disturbed the appearance of skirts and their wearers.

In January 1912 the feminists gathered en masse at the Palais Bourbon to demand

72.

votes for women as part of the new electoral system. They wore jackets and ankle-length gored skirts in grey, blue or dark green. They had thrown away the bustles which previously gave added shape to their behinds, but stumbled a little as they fled from the police because their skirts tapered towards the hem.

"Skirts" were not admitted to the elections to Germany's Reichstag, either. But the world kept on imperceptibly changing, women continued their transformations, and time-honoured traditions gradually gave way.

In China, General Yuan Shi Kai, clad in a kimono resplendent with a golden dragon, symbolically had his pigtail, an emblem of the past, cut off, while the revolutionary government proclaimed the nationalist republic. All the weekly magazines carried an engraving of the elegant, static, Empress of China. Her sumptuous satin-stitch embroideries on stiff silk tunics which combined violently contrasting colours captured the imagination of the French couturiers. Their oriental-style ladies wallowed in luxury, silk and pride. Erté's sophisticated outfits in lampshade-style, dripping with pearls, and pleated skirts with basques, followed in swift succession. Women were still torn between the two contrasting images available to them. Politics, or fragments of the family life of the unfortunate monarchs of the period influenced famous couturiers and obscure dressmakers alike. The news that Alexei, the Russian Tsarevich, was a haemophiliac leaked out from the court of St. Petersburg. The moving story of the bruises of the poor little prince who couldn't be allowed to play touched the hearts of aristocrats, the middle classes and the poor alike. Russia became fashionable. The tubular skirts which appeared beneath the long tunics fitted around the hips were called "à la Russe". They were all the rage in both summer and winter.

A fair number of them went to the bottom in the bowels of the Titanic, the world's biggest transatlantic liner, off the coast of Newfoundland. It was just before midnight when elegant ladies clad in satin skirts drawn in at the ankle went down

74. Women no longer had a doll-like image. The severe, softly flowing skirts in fashion in 1913 were a forewarning of astonishing revolutions. Their secret supports also changed: the foaming petticoats were replaced by straighter models in jersey, silk or *radium*, a new type of very light crepe de chine. *Mode Pratique* 1913.

dancing in small steps. The sounds of the orchestra couldn't mask the horrible crash of the "unsinkable" vessel against a huge iceberg.

ECLECTIC EXOTICISMS

A disconcerting variety of shapes were featured in fashions. Ideas and suggestions came not only from China and Russia but also from remotest Egypt. A sculpture of Queen Nefertiti was discovered during this period, and the fine, rhythmic ancient decorative motifs inspired artists and the couturiers, who placed elegant Egyptian friezes on the flounces of some skirts.

Exoticism was particularly fashionable in colonial Europe, whose citizens had access to fabrics, silver and bric-a-brac from different cultures at reasonable prices.

The fabrics were mysterious, shiny and brilliant. Silks, damasks and velvets were more common than flannel and cottons.

In October 1912 Mexico was in turmoil. The hero was Pancho Villa, who tried a coup d'état. The army was on the people's side and the women were with their menfolk. The uniform worn by the *soldaderas* of the revolutionary army which aimed to overthrow President Madeiro was unusual: ammunition belt, cartridge case, poncho and a full skirt in starched white cotton with three frills, decorated with vertical ribs and coarse lace. This skirt, typical of the Mexican folk tradition, was to appear on the fashion catwalks and the streets of the Twentieth Century on several occasions whenever clothing which looked suitable for a hot, hot summer was required.

ANKLE LENGTH SKIRTS
WITH BASQUE

On the eve of the First World War slightly shorter skirts were on view in towns. The image was stubbornly faithful to Poiret's ideology. The skirt was still ankle length but the hobble had disappeared and the stride was able to return to its natural length. The back, sides and bottom of the bobbin-shaped skirt featured little fan-shaped bands of pleats, allowing the legs to move. The few flat knife or box pleats featured were very discreet.

46

75. A sumptuous garden party *toilette*. The body and legs are enveloped in a draped, cross-over skirt. The fur trims emphasize the petal-shaped hemline.
Journal des dames et des modes 1913.

76.77. The affectionate meeting between a "dialect" skirt and the tapered skirt of a city-style suit.
Journal des dames et des modes 1913.
The imaginative elegance in vogue at the end of the Belle Epoque provided a daywear outfit consisting of a full skirt with its main colour matching a short bolero-jacket, and even a close-fitting cap. The elbow-length gloves are a final very sophisticated note. *Journal des dames et des modes* 1915.

78.79. Summer skirt in linen with large check pattern and semi-flowing line. The uneven hemline, longer at the back, leaves the ankles in view.
The shorter skirt in taffetta and striped silk voile with full loose pleats moves like a fluttering tunic over the tight-fitting sheath dress slightly tapered at the hem. *Journal des dames et des modes* 1914.

Shapes of clearly oriental inspiration were abandoned together with peacocks' feathers and useless frivolity. The preference was for softer fabrics which fell into folds.

A broad basque appeared on all skirts, emphasizing and slimming the line of the hips. Sometimes the *empiècement* took the shape of the bottom of a male waistcoat, with buttons and pocket, but more often it was a a bodice-like band decorated for the afternoon with dense overlapped drapery which gave the skirt a more striking appearance. In all cases the basque in fashion in 1914 differed from that in vogue in previous seasons, which reached almost up to the bust.

THE FUTURISTS IGNORE SKIRTS, AND A NEW CHAPTER STARTS

The silhouette of the skirt on the eve of the Great War slimmed the hips and featured a broader waistband, creating a high-waisted effect. The feet, clad in pointed shoes with curved heels, were still on view.

Literature and painting had made their mark on the art of dressing. It is strange to note that the Futurist movement, which made so much of "dynamic dressing" did not realise that the skirt had a great future before it, although they did design new clothing ideas. The movement of Marinetti and his companions came out in favour of striking clothes which broke with tradition: dresses with simplified structure, multi-coloured waistcoats and eye-catching shoes. But the group's documents make no mention of skirts, whether in solid colour or glittering shades, perhaps because in that period they were still considered unpretentious garments suitable for the lower classes, unworthy of the attention of intellectuals. The war against dull colours in skirts and dresses had started before 1915. Diaghilev, in the sets for his historic ballet productions, and Poiret in his sketches, both dipped their brushes in a wide range of colours which were rather shocking, at least at that time. "I have let loose a wild pack of wolves ... reds, greens and purples in the sheepfold full of women, who have

80,81. A highly elegant skirt in bordeau satin with a train which is wrapped round and fastened at the front with a "breloque" brooch.
To celebrate a family Christmas the modern lady wears a "chrysalis" line skirt which opens like a tight-fitting tunic over a pleated silk underskirt. *Journal des dames et des modes* 1914.

used elegance as an excuse for eliminating every hint of vitality from their wardrobes, suffocating under languide mauves, evanescent pinks and faded yellows." This was the warlike message put out by Poiret, who scented battles in the air and won his fight when ankles were displayed beneath hems in daring, bright colours.

The First World War forced humanity to start a new chapter. The maps and the female silhouette were both re-drawn. The blood-splashed suit worn by the Duchess of Hohenberg, bride of the Austrian Archduke, on that tragic day at Sarajevo in 1914 was still matronly, ankle length and softened by a few loose pleats. The hat, with its lofty ostrich plumes, was to remain securely attached to the head of the dying Archduchess by its pins. And this tragic image was to open a new era in the history of old Europe. Haughty feathers and skirts full of useless fripperies or which hampered movements were to disappear for ever.

49

82. A "chrysalis" line skirt features in this beetle-blue wool suit: the embroidered bodice-like waistband attaches the skirt to the blouse thanks to two buttons on the inside. *Mode illustrée*, 1915.

83. Cross-over straps for a Viennese style skirt in a hand-made fabric of Greek inspiration. Photograph by *Atelier d'Ora* 1917.

WARLIKE VARIATIONS
ON POCKETS

The skirts worn by the women who worked in factories left empty by the men called to the trenches provided various variations on the gored style, with pleats requiring pressing being eliminated for the sake of convenience. The fullness always started from the basque, and at this time skirts were ankle length. The fastening was at the back, with hooks, or at the front with a row of buttons. One detail: during the first years of the war the basque again started to rise towards the bust and skirts had a kind of "Empire" line. But this trend lasted' only a few seasons. At the end of 1916 and against the cannons' roar in 1917 fashions, which had stagnated for a decade as far as skirts were concerned, took another decisive step forward.

The new ideology in women's clothing was "practical is beautiful". Hemlines dared the impossible, rising by no less than 10 centimetres. High boots with long, densely buttoned fastenings carefully protected the legs from malicious or indiscreet eyes.

Boleros and swallow-tail coats were immediately replaced by comfortable

84. Skirts "at war" were those of the uniforms worn by the women who replaced the men in the public services. American ambulance drivers and members of the emigration service. *Pictorial Review* 1919.

safari jackets of clear military inspiration.

And when the United States of America also came into the conflict, women's magazines, especially American ones, offered readers skirts in abundance. The *Pictorial Review* addressed a very wide

85. Casual, practical skirts which were also fashionable and easy to wear even for those who had to go and work to replace the menfolk, who were still in the trenches in October 1917. *Pictorial Review*, 1917.

female public, so its fashion pages didn't show femmes fatales or vampiresses, or stereotyped models, but everyday women, decided and dynamic, worthy descendents of the pioneers of the West. Instead of silk fringes and wide strips of braid, they preferred the convenience of a well-designed pocket. Imaginations ran riot creating pockets large and small of all shapes and sizes: flap pockets, patch pockets, gathered pockets, heart or leaf shaped pockets, bellows pockets, frilled pockets and eyelet pockets.

WORK DOES NOT MAKE FOR NOBLE SKIRTS

Europe was changing face. Austria was becoming smaller and smaller. The female shape was also changing. The bust, which back in 1903 seemed to be supported on a tray, was reduced in size in 1910, being squashed almost to disappearance under flat blouses with no gathers or darts. Skirts puffed out at the sides until they took on the new "basket" shape. Side panels gores doubled in size, and huge triangular pockets hung to left and right. The women of Europe

had won their personal battle against restriction by skirts. Their movements became decided and energetic, very different from those of the era's latest great seductress, the dancer-spy Mata Hari who died before the firing squad in the wood at Vincennes in October 1917. She brought the age of mysterious, exotic women to a close. The curtain now went up on the world of work, and in Russia the first socialist society was being formed. This coincided with a celebration of working clothes. Then women's jobs were unskilled and did not give prestige which was strictly reserved for men but in spite of this, while the cannons roared dresses and skirts drew inspiration from working clothes. Skirts copied the style of aprons. Bibs, straps of various sizes and with or without cross-overs, skirts with built-in aprons and

86. The lines of the skirts which came from America in 1918 were slightly tapered at the hemline and gave just a hint of the "aubergine" shape with which the haute couture world was finally to accept shorter lengths after the First World War. Cross-cut panels with contrasting linings and two-button fastenings featured on the elegant skirt. Casual styles had practical but decorative pockets, soft, featured waistbands and diagonal motifs for winter: for summer they offered patch pockets, buttoned bows and uneven effect. *Pictorial Review* 1918.

Tyrolean-style skirts with *Schürtze* or *Tandelschürtze* all came in.

For the first time in the history of the working class, who had always followed blindly in the wake of the powerful when it came to fashions, they were able to set their mark on a clothing style where the keynote was functionality and pockets, straps, aprons and hems were the only decorative features.

THE BIG STORES

In 1919 on the old continent the watchword seemed to be "eliminate superstructures" and Walter Gropius, founder of the Bauhaus in Weimar, opened the history of "industrial art". Curves disappeared from the female body, while the line of the skirt provided a fine blend of the technical and the practical.

The belt, if present, moved down towards the hips. Pattern books showed women in relaxed poses, sometimes even with their hands in their pockets and their feet hinting at a dance step. A whole century seemed to have passed between these images and the sulky, coquettish attitudes struck by Belle Otero, the plump seductress of the *café-chantant* in Belle Epoque style.

The war was over and women were dancing to the sprightly rhythms of the foxtrot and one-step in black silk stockings. Marcel Proust received the Goncourt prize in an electric atmosphere very different from the shades and shadows inhabited by his young girls in bloom.

The unstoppable rise of the skirt as the

52

87. American magazines were also the source for the idea of skirts with new combinations of easy fit and attractive femininity. Aprons and bibs were derived from the Tyrolean costume, eye-catching checks enlivened the wear of busy housewives, and the straps with buttons looked like military styles. *Pictorial Review* 1918.

clothing of women in everyday life had begun. An important part in this was played by the big department stores, whose organizers realised that skirts

88. Silk, linen, cotton and light wool were the recommended fabrics for spring 1918. Skirts acquired greater character with giant checks, eye-catching stripes and full pockets. *Pictorial Review* 1918.

89. Gored skirt with buttoning motif on front worn by Miss De Wolfe, who had organized hospitals for fighting men in France during the war. *Vogue* 1918.

detached from bodices would be big business. No one could deny that skirts were easy to make and to wear, while dresses presented dressmakers with difficult technical problems. The complicated styles and unbalanced cuts required a lot of work and gave no guarantee of success. The problem of fit was overcome by dividing the dress into two separate parts which could be put together in different ways. The combination of skirt and blouse was immediately successful at all levels, meaning that the widest range of social classes were dressed all alike for the first time in history.

90. In 1919, almost as if the idea of elegance were extracting its revenge, skirts lengthened again and reached almost to the ankle. The practical features offered by the skirt, now indispensable in the female wardrobe, were guaranteed by the presence of pockets of all types, welt pockets, appliqué pockets, bellows pockets, double pockets, triple pockets and pouch pockets. *Pictorial Review* 1919.

STRIPES AND TARTANS

In the 1910s the variety of colours and types of fabric used in the production of skirts was astonishing, reflecting the uncertainty about the exact form this garment was to take.

During the first few years, for the "chrysalis" line skirts, the preference was for dry handle wool which did not go out of shape and which showed up the hobble shape clearly: wool serge, gabardine or crepe.

During the first world war the fabrics became lighter weight to give movement

91. Woollen cloths for walking out suits and for sporting outfits. The favourite fabrics were English wools and those produced in the Biella textile mills.

to the hang of gores and to the new flared line. Small stripes, small tartan patterns, cottons or wool cloth were in vogue.

At the end of 1918 the great revolution in the skirt's length had already taken place. For summer it could be in sateen printed with circus-style red and white stripes, or striking printed or yarn-dyed tartan fabrics and the so-called Vichy cloths, so that even the material emphasized the idea that "skirt equals worker's overall" so dear to this era of social renewal.

92. Variations on the pocket theme for working skirts. *Pictorial Review* 1919.

56

THOSE ROARING TWENTIES

SKIRTS IN THE TWENTIES

The 1914-1918 war passed over the female figure like a steamroller. Curves were flattened, but spirits were unaffected and the conflict brought forward women with a lively independence of mind who, once they had got into the offices and factories to replace the men called to arms, had no wish to leave them again. The number of women teachers, hospital staff, civil servants and freelance workers increased everywhere.

Female workers began to gravitate towards the service sector. In the same way, women who had previously been maids of all work and who had been placed in factories during the war refused to go back to their old jobs when the conflict came to an end. During the Twenties, as the statistics show, in the U.S.A., Austria, Germany, France and England the reduction in the number of domestic servants was dramatic. Women who had experienced regular working hours didn't want to become servants and even preferred temporary unemployment.

The skirt was now worn regularly and at all levels. The new, very simple design lengthened and slimmed the figure, just as it appears in Modigliani's portraits. Hemlines were 20-25 cm above the floor. The tightly buttoned boots had disappeared, making way for shoes with buckles and heels. There were no belts at the waist, and the collarless blouses were worn on the outside, like short tunics.

Skirts with straps and bibs were worn on summer mornings in the home or while gardening. Pleated skirts for different

93. Two shades of pink, pale yellow, mandarin and violet combine on the silk muslin overskirt worn over a crepe sheath dress to transform it into a stunning filmy ball-dress. *Femina* 1929.

sports, for strolls in town and for travelling were made more individual by variations in cut and colour. Naturally a skirt and blouse provided the most convenient clothing for wear beneath the shiny black cotton sateen overall for office work of all kinds. The female students who had recently been admitted to all the world's universities and high schools, and considered themselves "emancipated", even if they were almost always accompanied to and from school, wore skirts which were generally pleated, with knife or box plates, with a knitted jacket fastened with buttons which, in the U.S.A., generally carried the badge of their college.

Flowing, unsymmetrical skirts were reserved for brilliant social occasions, where they reflected the wish to let oneself go and transgress. There were two adjectives, "crazy" and "roaring", used to describe the passion for luxury and wild living which ran through the world after the First World War. A new snobbery came into clothes,

94. Thin detached panels fluttered and waved to the wearer's dance steps, while uneven cuts, petal effects or spiral looks interrupted the cut of semi-fitted skirts reaching just below the knee. *Femina* 1920.

95. The elegant suit consisted of a little velvet jacket with a bell-shaped skirt gathered on the hips. The clear stripes on the serge fabric look like a braided embroidery. *Femina* 1920.

behaviour and drink. The champagne so dear to the "viveurs" of the Belle Epoque was now replaced by whisky or gin. This era also saw the triumph of Bitter Campari, Cinzano vermouth, Punt-e-Mes, Carpano and the Martini, a cocktail which went by the name of the Italian vermouth used to make it. The impression is that women of the period had always to be doing two things at once in order to feel dynamic, modern and emancipated: they sipped the new cocktails while smoking cigarettes in very long holders. They went for strolls wearing wool jersey skirts which followed the shape of the body without clinging and without hindering their steps, holding the lead of a dog of the most fashionable breed, a black, bristly Scottish terrier. During spins in the motor car, skirts billowed in the breeze created and ladies read magazines published especially for them, while in America, during the Prohibition, they took secret sips from hidden flasks.

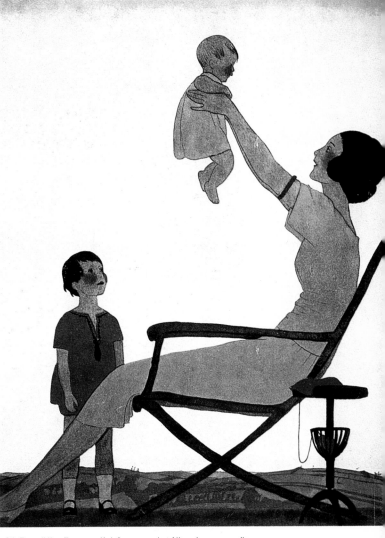

96.

96. For all the "housewifely" moments of the day, a woollen skirt with a slightly full waistline tapering towards the hem. *Femina* 1920.

FOXTROT

This was also the era of a young, exciting, fresh musical style, the foxtrot. In 1922 the music critic, Hervé Lauwick, wrote from Paris that "you have to like the foxtrot, because it's a product of our times. When its melody ceases, you realize how much happiness it contained."

While Europe was giving itself up to the new dance, in the United States another musical form was becoming known: jazz, which originated in New Orleans. Louis Armstrong and Sidney Beckett reigned supreme. Their melodies provided dancing music for young people in the U.S.A. and were eagerly awaited by members of the same age-group in the old continent. While

97.

97. The pleated skirt was almost a uniform on the beaches frequented by international high society in the Twenties. *Femina* 1920.

98. Madame Lucien Lelong wears an almond green circular skirt with the front hanging in a deep slanting fold. *Femina* 1923.

dancing, girls dangled long cherry earrings. Hair was sacrificed to hygiene and convenience. The new very short cut which left the nape of the neck bare was called the *garçonne* style. Strangely, hair lengths seemed to follow hemlines as they became short, very short, fringed, uneven, zig-zag and wavy. Hemlines wavered around the knee, moving up or down every six months. For evening wear, or for long bridal gowns, the ankles and the pretty strapped shoes ready for marking time to the beat of dancing music were always in view.

ART DECO

In 1925, the vital year for the Art Déco movement, the exhibition of decorative arts was opened in Paris. This was the greatest artistic event of the postwar period and the definitive consecration of the luxury articles of the roaring Twenties. The designs were based on the circle, the triangle and the square. Clothes and prints adapted to the idea, with thin, flowing

99. A new clothing style was the pleated crepe overskirt fastened with a strip of gold braid like an apron. *La mode pratique* 1924.

fabrics in the forefront. Knitted skirts (machine knitted) featured thin stripes, zig-zags, and mélange effects in a number of shades. The same year saw the outbreak of the craze for the Charleston, the dance which supplanted the one-step. To dance it, young people had to have even more skill and more agility at knee level than for the paso-doble. The skirts of dresses were very low waisted, and were formed of frills or flares. The legs naturally remained in view and commonly held ideas about modesty were offended. Moralizing campaigns were launched all over the world, criticizing short skirts, thighs on show, the Charleston and all the rest.

Although the mood of the times required that fashions should give women a more masculine air (flat chests, very short hair and male habits like smoking and drinking), more feminine notes came through in everyday life and in grammar. The motor car, which had hitherto been treated as a masculine noun in Italian grammar, changed sex thanks to Gabriele D'Annunzio, who stated in a letter to Giovanni Agnelli senior

that "it has the grace, the slenderness and the vivacity of a seductress, so the automobile must be considered as feminine."

Wealthy girls became emancipated under the aegis of the goddess Speed and acquired driving licences. Their poorer sisters attended shorthand and typing courses which made their fingers fly faster than the wind. It's wonderful to "handle" a machine, whether for transport or writing.

Sports were within the reach of a large proportion of the public and even the least elitist and extravagant sports developed their own clearly defined uniform during these years.

In 1926 *Femina* magazine carried a series of very sophisticated tennis outfits. There could be nothing more seductive than playing with racquet and ball clad in a white ensemble with a slight touch of red and blue or green and blue. Patou offered a knee-length skirt in which smooth panels were interspersed with bands of narrow pleats, with matching tunic and white cardigan. The same skirt could also be worn with a tunic featuring a square neckline. A skirt with pleated panels featuring a zig-zag hem was more daring and original, but very elegant.

100.

100. In these years it seemed that skirts just had to be pleated. For spring or summer they were in light silk fabrics such as crepe de chine, shantung and crepe georgette, in pleats of various kinds. *Vogue* 1926.

101.

101. The comfortably elegant interior of the new Buick toned in very well with a gabardine suit with box-pleated skirt. The tight-fitting *cloche* hat and the gloves and two-colour shoes complete the driver's dynamic style. *Femina* 1928.

102.

103.

104.

102.103.104. In 1925 skirts suddenly became shorter to the very limits set by the modesty of the period. White, as it had to be for tennis, the skirt was given movement by a draped panel on the hip. In 1926 the French couturiers took a look at sports clothes. Jean Patou offered a skirt with groups of pleats which formed little grooves, while Groupy created a "zig-zag" hemline for a silk crepe tennis skirt.

For yachting, skirts had to be in jersey. The shape was also important: they were slightly flared or straight cut to prevent a naughty wind from raising the hem. For the real Amazons, in 1927 the German magazine *Die Dame* suggested very short divided skirts in woollen cloth with a leather belt round the waist to match the boots.

At about the time of the death of Isadora Duncan, the great innovator in the dance world who appeared on stage barefoot, a new famous woman, Coco Chanel, was taking her place on the fashion scene. Her motto, "real chic means seeming expensively poor", astonished the Parisians.

Poiret's star was on the wane. The new break with tradition offered by Coco Chanel, the designer who apart from anything else came from a very humble

106.

105. For the small Mediterranean cruise here are two extraordinary couture skirts. Jane Régny decorated the skirt in white kasha with uneven cuts and insets low on the hips emphasized by buttons, while the other model in blue satin crepe featured a motif of two-colour triangles. *Femina* 1929.

106. Each sport had its skirt. For rowing it had to be white, lightweight, and flared or pleated. *Femina* 1925.

107. Yet more pleats in this shooting outfit: the skirt, in very lightweight loden, consists of three pleated flounces which makes it suitable for any society shooting occasions. *Femina* 1928.

105.

107.

108.

background and had no family tree to support her, left people perplexed. Her ideas were very clear and her will stronger than steel. Coco Chanel's suits were immediately seen to be revolutionary: they featured straight ordinary or wrap-over skirts whose length never changed over the years and decades: just a little below the knee. The jackets were reduced to a minimum, with over them a cascade of chains and jewels worn casually as if they were worthless trinkets. Chanel imposed other dictates: the pockets of a skirt must always be in a position accessible to the hands; a skirt button, if provided, must fasten, and skirts must above all be easy to walk in, even tapered ones, which were therefore provided with slits, kick-pleats or gores.

Her favourite materials for skirts were often untidy and unravelled looking, and glowed with muted colour. It was no coincidence that this great designer was the first to appreciate the beauty of the fabrics produced at Prato from waste wool,

108. For lunch at the club house of the golf course at Touquet, Jeanne Lanvin offered the sophisticated lady a soft two piece in *crepe marocain* with gored skirt cut on the bias figured with little horizontal folds, or a lighter more dynamic model with the pleats stitched down at the front. *Femina* 1929.

109. For skiing, even if suitable trousers had already made their appearance, a real lady still wore skirts such as this one by Jeanne Lanvin, featuring a very original rounded yoke and superimposed panel. *Femina* 1929.

110. "Curling" arrived from America. The correct outfit consisted of a short skirt in heavy tweed with one side flared and the other with flat pressed pleats. *Femina* 1929.

109.

110.

which gave clothes an elegant, lived-in air. She made use of them, and kept their origins a secret.

All this practicality, naturalness and the mixing of the male and female spirits overturned the concepts which formed the basis of the impeccable international haute couture styles, and these are principles still perfectly valid and up to date after more than half a century, even during the interlude in 1928, when fashions underwent a considerable change.

The theme "fullness on the back of the figure" met with the approval of most couturiers. They seemed to have reached an agreement all together, but in reality they all designed in secrecy, locked away in their "ateliers" in Paris which were as inaccessible as fortresses. The overloaded

111. Coco Chanel in 1920, wearing a practical and elegant light-coloured sporting skirt fastened right down the side by a row of buttons.

112. Philippe e Gaston offered a white skirt in *kasha* featuring two inserted panels cut on the bias with rounded hem which add a graceful touch of movement to the front. *Femina* 1929.

111.

112.

line of the 1880s, which seemed to provide the inspiration for the fashions of 1928-9, created skirts rich in art, technique and taste.

The concentration of the fullness at the back meant that the front had to be simplified. Draperies or simple flowing gores hung unevenly towards the back, on the side or hip. In 1929 skirts took a decided step forward along the difficult but elegant path of applied decorations, which were to be further developed during the years immediately afterwards.

THE FABRICS

Modernism and the wish for a very long silhouette like that shown in the paintings of Van Dongen led creators to use fabrics which did not add bulk. The ideal cloth

113. Fashion had preferences even when it came to dogs. In the Twenties terriers were all the rage. Probably their small size and energetic appearance matched the style of the casual clothes of the time. A very elegant green wool skirt with parallel stitching to emphasize its straight cut is here shown with fox terrier. By Jane Régny. *Jardin des modes* 1929.

66

MADAME ET SON CHIEN
Ensemble de JANE RÉGNY

clung to the body without pulling it in, caressing and emphasizing lines without rounding them. The new tubular knitting machines flung open the door to a highly successful fabric: jersey. Woven fabrics with Indian or Persian designs, those with dense, complicated patterns, bulky, heavy woollen cloths and D'Annunzian fabrics seemed to belong to the far distant past. There was a lot of enthusiasm for light crepes and wool knits enlivened by gold stripes. Rodier renamed their fabrics *kasha* or *djersa* or *kasharisa*, names which suggested inviting, exotic, non-existant islands.

Towards 1928 fabrics tended to have a stiffer handle. For summer heavy shantung silk, perhaps in Nile green, was in fashion, while winter styles used velvets in bright solid colours or dotted with large multicolour lozenges.

114. The bias-cut "shaped" inset in this very elegant skirt by Maggy Rouff takes up the whole front, giving the garment an unusually soft appearance. Jane Régny prefers a light-coloured skirt with wide flat-pressed pleats. *Femina* 1929.

115. During the Twenties, and especially towards the end of the decade, the skirt was given more and more precise roles. The brilliant *habituées* of the Hotel Majestic in Cannes wore "tailored" skirts with pointed cuts and insets and deep kick-pleats during the riviera winter season beneath a variety of coats. *Femina* 1929.

114.

115.

116. The Chantal and Schiaparelli skirts show the delicacy of their cut both in the welt pocket inserted in the seam of the front pleat and in the two diamond-shaped buttons which fasten the straight panel on the bias-cut skirt.

THE DISILLUSIONED CALM
1930-1940

IN SEARCH OF REASSURANCE

At the beginning of the 1930s the bust, waistline and hips were all indicated, cut and sewn in their natural places. The starting point for the creation of an outfit consisting of a skirt with a short jacket were the female figure and its attributes: a slim, supple, sweet figure. The Thirties preferred the reassuring seductiveness of a curved line to the jumpy, nervous straight lines which had characterized the Art Déco woman of 1925.

And reassurance was really required. The tremendous Wall Street Crash of 1929 had come like a bolt from the blue to hit all those involved with the stock markets, the wild heroes of Fitzgerald's novels, and ordinary mortals too. Its effects spread to Europe, where it also caused fears and anxiety.

Fashions, which are more intelligent than many people think, got the message and adapted their rules. They used a calm image to try to create an atmosphere of order and security, exactly like the three ideologies, Fascism, Nazism and Francoism, which were accumulating more and more supporters in a world torn by opposite and incompatible trends.

If aggression was the dominant note in the political life of the Thirties, with the extreme right and the extreme left meeting in bloody cruelty, sweetness was the "leit-motiv" of fashion, which had abandoned all ideas of breaks with the past, challenges and provocations.

117. The movement in this white silk skirt cut in gores is provided by the central gore, which is a triangle inserted upside down. The belt and rectangular buckle are covered with the same material as the sophisticated casual outfit itself. *Femina* 1930.

Skirts, which in 1929 had dedicated themselves to the irregularities of uneven panels and jagged, disturbing hemlines, now chose the path of moderation and quiet creative work. Imagination seemed to be as strictly controlled as fullness, length and fit.

Tranquil but sublime skirts appeared in the fashion magazines. The cut, or rather cuts, dominated the scene from morning to afternoon, showing basques with textbook applied decorations.

If an idea or whim did come to the surface, it had to be sober, unshowy, and noticeable only close to. On a line which remained faithful to a very moderate slight flare with a flowing hang, the band below the waist might be decorated with zig-zag

118. Casual gored skirts in wool jersey with flare at the hem by Jeanne Lanvin. *Femina* 1930.

120. At the "villes d'eau" or spa towns recommended wear was a "patterned" two-piece ensemble in silk. The skirts always featured pleats or tucks, intarsia or applied panels and bands cut on the bias. *Femina* 1930.

119.

119. The skirt of the green loden suit by "chez Rochas" is cut in the shape of wide pleats. *Fémina,* 1930.

118

120.

graphic stitching, fabric appliqués resembling the pattern of a parquet floor, or meandering parallel lines which first ran round below the waist and then crossed over like a modern motorway interchange on one hip.

It was the great moment of basques and of rounded pleats for sportswear. Skirts of the period had an unexpected elegance communicated by ribs, bands of pleats and intarsia work.

PRETENTIOUS PROTAGONISTS

In 1931-32, women loved skirts which were "masterpieces of tailoring". For the first time in the history of the world, it was discovered that a good skirt must fit just as well as, or perhaps better than, a good dress. The skirt was no longer just for casual wear, and it was felt that it had been unfair to relegate it to the lower rungs of clothing's social ladder. So the doors were flung open to the new skirt, the leading

121.

121. Viyella, a light wool fabric with a soft handle, became a classic in the Thirties. It was washable and non-shrink and proved to be the unreplaceable ideal fabric, especially for skirts for sports, for morning wear, for the country and for sports. *Le Jardin des modes* 1931.

122. Grey flannel skirt cut almost straight. Typical of billions of similar skirts which inhabited the wardrobes of women the world over. *Le Jardin des modes* 1931.

122.

figure in the modern wardrobe and with pretentions to elegance set out in today's terms: hand-knitted sweater and casual skirt; a short jacket or bolero worn over a skirt with an elaborate basque; or for summer a simple shirt plus a linen skirt with pleats or clearly marked seams.

The length during these years was that accepted by common consensus as best: below the knee. Extravagantly or excessively tight or full skirts were not acceptable: they were just full enough to allow women to stride out and walk up and down steps without problems. The skirt, like the architecture of the time, became rational and shunned unwanted artifices or decorations. The fabrics with a warm, soft handle for winter were alternated, for summer wear, with crisp fibres such as linen, whose snowy whiteness provided a better background for the crafted perfection of intarsia work.

NEW FASHION LENGTHS

It was in 1932 that Jean Patou decreed from Paris that the new ideal length for

123. For the first misty mornings of autumn, Burberry's, the raincoat specialists, offered a divided skirt and a blouse in waterproof fabric. Révillon, another "maison" which produced very casual clothes, suggested a wrap-over skirt fastened with four buttons. *Le jardin des modes* 1932.

124. A parade of skirts for 1931. *Le jardin des modes* 1931.

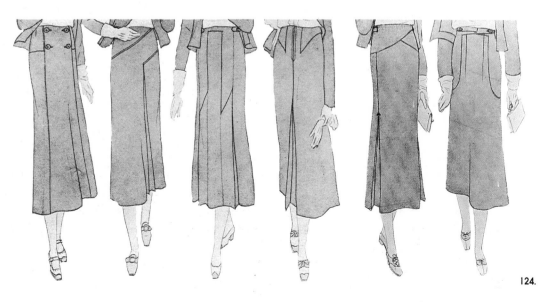

124.

125.126. In 1932 skirts reached down to mid calf length and were worn over decidedly high heels to create a more streamlined figure. *Lidel* 1932.

Polcki

skirts for morning and afternoon wear was mid-calf. For evening and bridal gowns, hemlines were ordered to abandon their position around the ankle and aim decidedly for the floor. This revolution was immediately accepted by all couturiers, including the Italians, who allowed themselves to be seduced by the new length. At that time the capital of good taste was Turin. This was the birthplace of the Ente Nazionale della Moda (National Fashion Authority), which had to produce propaganda for an image of international elegance at a time of sanctions.

The national beacon projected a style whose keynote was respectabiity, and whose main features were excellent quality fabrics in discreet colours with a lukewarm handle, and making-up which was faultless both on the surface and in all the hidden finishings. This was also the period of reversible fabrics, which offered considerable technical problems. During the early Thirties the skirt

and all garments produced by Piedmontese elegance were made with painstaking stitches which had nothing to fear from even the most thorough inspection. In fact, purchasers generally turned them inside out to check the finishing on the inside: as in a perfect piece of embroidery, the wrong side had to be as impeccable as the right.

Patou's new longer length skirt had more flow. The artifice and intarsia on the basque were abandoned in favour of the elegance of a gored skirt which hugged the hips and then opened out into a moderate fullness which swung at each step. In autumn, for wear with contrasting jackets, there were also fishtail skirts fitted to the knee and then finishing in one very full flounce. The favourite colour was still white, the symbol of purity and perfection.

127. For beachwear, a skirt in striped cloth with wrap-over fastening featuring double panel at the back. *Le Jardin des modes* 1932.

128. The alternative to the wrap-over skirt for beachwear was this figured linen design. Another idea for the summer skirt was the knickerbockers design caught in below the knee. Drawing by R. Gruau, *Lidel* 1933.

74

127.

128.

129. Gored or shaped-cut skirts which all hang very straight thanks to their wool jersey fabric, which was used increasingly frequently. *Le jardin des modes* 1934.

130. For afternoon appointments the strongly patriotic magazine *Dea* offered a *redingotta* trimmed with *agnello di Persia* for wear over a slightly flared skirt in purple *lanital* and a suit with skirt fastened at the front down to the hips with an opening which resembled a pleat. *Dea* 1936.

INSPIRATION FROM THE CINEMA

The international film star industry was becoming an important social phenomenon in those years. The star of a German film set in post-war Germany was a pale but stunning blonde who was previously completely unknown: her name was Marlene Dietrich. Her way of moving, her gestures and her film-star suits with stylized skirts immediately caught on. The stores of dreams were written on the reels of black and white film. Mountains of light, inoffensive, escapist films built castles in the air and invented comical/sentimental mix-ups. Italy's film capital was Turin, and the films made there won the nickname of "i film dei telefoni bianchi" ("white telephone films") because of their soothing plots and upper middle class settings.

While the streets outside rang to the Nazi goose-step and the songs of the Fascist blackshirts, in the dark of the cinema people were magically transported into fantastic, luxurious surroundings. A world of exquisite fashions passed before the viewers' ingenuous eyes. The screen became the master of life and images. Now every woman knew how to dress for a *soirée*, to go to friends' houses for tea (or rather carcadé) or to stroll "lazily beneath the lukewarm sky, enchanted by all that light and the implacable blue of the sky and sea" (*Lidel* 1932).

AS LONG AS IT'S WHITE

At that time fashion reports from Paris were offered alongside national fashion coverage with the skilful illustrations of a magician of the drawing world, René Gruau, whose work first appeared in the Italian magazine *Lidel*. Couturiers, designers and journalists rushed in a body to promulgate the undeniable super-elegance of dressing in white. At this point it is really appropriate to underline how

1   2

130.

administrative sector and to forbid married women from working in the public services in 1933.

In 1936 things were taken to extremes, with "studies on the pathology of women's work" providing details of all the horrible illnesses which might strike women in offices and factories. But there was another even more significant point: in Mussolini's Italy a woman was paid 50% less for doing exactly the same job as a man.

So skirts, whose most important feature was that they were practical, quick garments forming part of interchangeable outfits allowing a different combination to be used every day, lost ground.

They lost the pockets which were highly practical containers for women forced to spend long hours outside the home. Tight-waisted skirts, so uncomfortable for long hours spent sitting behind a desk, were back.

131. What could be better for car journeys than a slightly flared wool skirt? *Le Jardin des modes* 1937.

132. Fashionable holiday-makers wore practical skirts, sometimes divided. *Le Jardin des modes* 1937.

131.

this delicate non-colour, which requires a lot of care and demands painstaking maintenance, comes back to the forefront every time women are pushed out of the world of work for political and economic reasons. On this occasion, this meant that they had ample time to remove stains from, bleach, wash, starch and iron the impeccable white skirts with loose pleats, in gores or godets, which they were asked to wear.

The Fascist regime's demographers considered that the presence of women in the workforce (undertaking work outside the home) was "undermining the birthrate" and so, in their opinion, all the fair sex's "disgust" for such activities must be aroused.

Mussolini had already had laws passed to limit the employment of women in the

132.

FASCIST WOMEN AND FASCIST SKIRTS

The figure was still long and slender, in spite of all the right-wing ideologues who insisted that woman's first mission in life was as guardian of the home. The role of the Fascist woman was proclaimed in a speach by the DUCE (the title had to be written in capital letters) on 20th June 1937. "Women must be responsible for the early education of their offspring, whom we wish to be numerous and healthy. The generations of warriors and soldiers required for the defence of the empire will be as you women are capable of making them." So they were being offered a subordinate role, as breeding stock. "A mother who has children must have majestically wide hips, to avoid problems during childbirth," *Lidel* stated (1932). But, as is well known, this physical attribute does not make for an elegant line and causes problems for any item of clothing. The ingenuity of the designers at this crucial moment of history was ready and waiting to solve the problem by creating a kind of full-fitting skirt, cleverly cut to lengthen and give grace to the female figure and concealing the defects which the fanatics saw as maternal virtues.

The models suggested in the magazines of the period were all figure-slimming skirts which rested on round hips without emphasizing them, slid over large behinds, caressed the thighs without revealing their dimensions and stopped at mid calf length, the ideal for prolonging the vertical effect of the line. These skirts were perfect for any woman a few pounds overweight, with a wrap-over fastening giving ease of movement and slimming the figure, and repeated lines of vertical stitching to create a wholly illusory slenderness.

The "fascist" skirt as such was seen in the thronging crowds beneath the famous balcony in Piazza Venezia in Rome. This was a black wool skirt, with deep 5 cm pleats running from right to left, held down by stitching on the hips. They were 45 cm from the ground, shorter for the

133. The female uniforms required by Fascist fashions provided "giovani italiane" and "piccole italiane" with black skirts featuring pleats 5 or 8 cm wide.

"piccole italiane" and "figlie della lupa", who paraded behind the banner, marching in step every saturday afternoon.

Mens sana in corpore sano was the motto proclaimed by the herolds of the regime, and all, or almost all, women of the right age, whether or not they wanted to, took part in some form of athletics. However, female modesty, middle-class morality and freedom of movement had in some way to be reconciled. Someone (who has remained anonymous) attempted this. Schools were invaded by a strange hybrid design of pleated divided skirts, held in place by two intractable elastic bands below the knee. The rounded shape reached almost halfway down the leg, giving an unpleasant lamp-shade effect. This garment was used by girls at "physical education" lessons in all Italian schools for exercises on the wall-bars.

The female athletes of the Farnesina trained for throwing the javelin wearing pleated white divided skirts of knee length. Tennis players had a very different style: Claretta Petacci played doubles at the Camilluccia wearing pleated skirts in spotless white linen.

SHORES AND BEACHES:
MIDDLE-CLASS HOLIDAYS

Between 1935 and 1938 the middle classes discovered the beach. Dutiful mothers took children dreaming of a pistacchio, lemon and strawberry flavour ice-cream, whose hair had been scraped into place with a wet comb, for walks along the sea front. The mothers themselves would never have dreamed of walking around eating an ice-cream, even if it was in the colours of the Italian flag. They wore the new modern sundresses with low necklines, and straight skirts cut on the bias for wear with knitted tops. The pareo-skirts were clearly of Abyssinian inspiration, while those which were gored or pleated throughout were pulled in at the waist with tie-fastenings. At the beginning of the Thirties the seaside fashion was for very long gored skirts in shapes which showed the curves of the figure.

This fashion was inconvenient, if striking, because the over-long skirt dragged in the

134. Glamourous, seductive long striped cotton skirt in the same material as the "two-piece" bathing costume. Very elegant wear for fashionable beaches.
Le jardin des modes 1937.

135. A curious idea for the beach girl: very short divided skirt in navy blue cloth cut with panels of pleats inserted on the hips and decorated with unusual square buttons.
Le jardin des modes 1936.

134.

135.

136. The favourite summer fashion wear for the seaside was a shorter than normal skirt over shorts or a swimsuit, knotted at the front. *Femina* 1939.

137. The draped skirt fastened at the front looks like a pareo and is of clear Abyssinian origin. *Dea* 1938.

sand. The sailor theme proved itself the most appropriate for wear in seaside resorts: white or blue figured linen skirts decorated with gilded buttons featuring an anchor motif.

More buttons, in bamboo shape, emphasized wrap-over skirts and never-ending fabric buttons provided the back fastening for the flared, decidedly long skirts.

PLAYING AT SHEPHERD GIRLS

In 1938 history was on the brink of the Second World War and skirts took on less sugary styles and forms. Fashions for middle-class women took on more aggressive connotations.

Hemlines suddenly shot up to the knee, shapes became fuller and in many cases the hemlines of the flared skirts in woollen cloth were decorated with Tsarina-style trimmings, although these were in in moleskin, not sable, in view of the political

138. Brunetta, the great fashion designer, suggested this skirt with straps in cotton with parallel ribbings which provide a fitted waist and a frill beneath the bust. For country holidays. *Grazia* 1939.

139. A wardrobe consisting of two skirts, three blouses and a jacket, which was able to provide all the elegance required for daytime and afternoon wear. *Le jardin des modes* 1939.

divided up by a series of sunray ribbons, provided an attractive contrast with the whole colour of the tube skirt worn beneath them. For summer walks, they were completed by pretty "Little Red Riding Hood" wicker baskets perhaps as an attempt on women's part to exorcise their fears of what was happening around them by pretending to be innocent and unworried.

For evening wear the glamour of the gathered, bow-covered frill triumphed over more sober styles in France. The gaily flared skirts were decorated with pleated edges which fluttered at every step, revealing glimpses of the red satin ribbons sewn inside them.

The autumn-winter 1939 season saw the launch in Paris of an unusual evening ensemble: a long tartan skirt in loosely pleated alpaca with a hint of a train, worn with a black jacket and long gloves. France was already at war and the skirt was using its well-known versatility to adapt to providing evening elegance under emergency conditions.

situation. Colour combinations did not shy away from decided, eye-catching contrasts. Blue revealed a fire-red lining to a pleat. Winter skirts for wear with over-jackets were in heavy wool fabric, gored, and unexpectedly full, just covering the knee.

In 1939, when the cannons were already roaring, couture houses indulged themselves with a fashion inspired by "shepherdesses". Elegant ladies transformed themselves into carefree peasant girls just like Marie Antoinette's friends on the eve of the French Revolution, wearing short gathered skirts with laced filk-style bodices. To make their skirts stand out, they had no hesitation in wearing petticoats full of lace and starched sangallo frills, often in full view because a fold of the skirt was carelessly hooked up at the waist. So grandmother's *jupons* and cheerful countrified petticoats in red and white checked cotton were back in fashion.

The flowered cotton fabrics of full apron-skirts, gathered at the waist or

140. Slightly flared blue skirt with grey pleat. Model by Lucien Lelong. *Femina* 1939.

SILK AND SELF-SUFFICIENCY

The combination of the slightly flared skirt and collarless shirt, both in jersey, opened new horizons to the freer clothing style which followed the body's movements. Wool crepe's hang, handle and light weight permitted it to dominate the winter scene together with tricot made on the new tubular knitting machines. In Italy, it was called *maglina*, all foreign words being taboo. In summer the preference was for linen, which emphasized gored or loosely pleated skirts with a cool elegance. When it came to fabrics for tailored suits for autumn wear, the favourite choice was narrow stripes

141. Nina Ricci combines a gored skirt with fur trim at the hem with the sumptuous elegance of a squirrel jacket and muff. *Femina* 1939.

142. Balenciaga trims the hem of this elegant black taffetta skirt with double frill and two satin bows which peep out as if from a petticoat. *Femina* 1939.

143. Unusual evening wear: long skirt in tartan wool alpaca with pleats at the back and a hint of a train. *Femina* 1939.

142.

Veste et manchon de petit gris Jupe à godets bordée de fourrure

141.

143.

144. The long, tight-fitting skirt slightly flared at the hem and buttoned throughout its length provides a streamlined, graceful silhouette. Model by Nina Ricci. *Femina* 1938.

145. The divided skirt was more and more fashionable, especially during those years when riding a bicycle and freedom of movement were real necessities. From a Sormani drawing of the Forties.

in thousands of combinations of black and white or grey and white, and small or medium sized checks cut on the cross to give a better fit on the hips. However, a touch of white in flannel or alpaca was never lacking amidst all those gloomy shades.

For elegant afternoon or evening wear silk velvet, sumptuous and sweet, was used in association with faille, which had more body. This was also the period which saw the appearance of the fabrics of self-sufficiency: strange hempen cloths produced from fibres from the wild broom plant, and man-made silks derived from rayon which were given attractive names such as *romantrene*, *crespo Griselda* and *solidene* and used for lighter, more flared skirts.

Sheep's wool was replaced by a substitute woven from a derivate of milk: this slippery, cold flannel which was used to clothe Italian self-sufficiency was called *lanital*.

Pure silk shantung and toussor, the leading characters in the first summers of the Thirties, were confined, for economic reasons, to the most select wardrobes.

Cottons of all kinds and qualities played the leading role when it came to skirts large and small: "caroline", zephyr, gingham, muslin, canvas and chintzes of every conceivable colour, with more garish colours towards the end of the decade, and a wide variety of multi-coloured striped, checked and polka-dot designs.

144.

NECESSITY IS THE MOTHER
OF ... FASHION
1940 - 1950

145.

RECYCLED ELEGANCE

As soon as war broke out skirts became simpler and shorter, eliminating all complicated cuts and super-structures because, as we have already noted, skirt styles are clearly linked to women's social condition. Once again, the fair sex was called upon to replace men, whether willingly or by force of circumstances. When the bombs started to drop the mystique of femininity evaporated. Women worked in factories and became ticket-collectors, tram-drivers or nurses. Another reason behind the change in the silhouette was the shortage of fabric. Women tried to express optimism and happiness, at least in colours. White seemed empty and lifeless.

During the dark years of the war the spontaneous art of recycled elegance flourished. Outmoded dresses and coats were recycled, provided they were of precious wool, to become garments with a modern, shorter, and more casual cut. Flannels were worn with herring-bone patterns, tweeds and cavallery twills, woollen cloths and furs, army blankets and ancient corduroys.

Men's trousers in the practically unobtainable, crush-resistant English wool changed sex thanks to a few vertical seams emphasized by ribbing or stitching. They became tight four-panel skirts which had a certain line, even if the expert eye was able to tell their origin.

Tailors and dressmakers were busy providing intarsia work on half-fronts, pockets and hems: skirts sported herringbone basques, waistcoat style, produced from male lapels. The tiny apron-style patch pockets decorating the fronts of the flared skirts were made from old cuffs. Even famous couturiers constructed masterpieces which complied with this law of combination: fabrics and offcuts of the widest possible variety of origins were paired off with results which were far from unpleasant, even if invariable multicoloured.

Skirts with added flounces in contrasting colours appeared, especially for growing girls, as did those which alternated horizontal stripes of widely different fabrics. Checked light wools gave a younger touch to dark iron grey woollen cloths. For evening wear, the ideology of hybridisation

produced striking flared skirts which alternated bands of fabric with lace flounces.

In spite of the tragedy of the war itself, the food shortages and the difficulties in communications there was no decrease in female vanity, which was quick to respond to the new situation. The "unthinkable"

146. Elegant skirts: the fashion for skirts and blouses was logical and practical in wartime. In wool, knitted or in velvet, they are decorated with draped frills or gathers. *Fili Moda* 1944.

147. Casual skirts: simple and so handy for evacuations, cycling and for shopping, always a trying business. "Patterned" fabrics, wool tricot and heavy cloths with deep pleats, panels and fulnesses. They looked good with "men's" shirts. *Fili moda* 1944.

combination of a raincoat, an eminently sporting garment, with an informal evening skirt was worn for cycling to the theatre.

INGENIOUS RESOURCEFULNESS

Wartime fashions drew on thousands of other resources to provide imaginative, attractive solutions to the problems posed by the limitations imposed. Since it was impossible to walk through town in a long skirt without attracting curious glances, someone invented a short skirt to which an extra flounce reaching down to the ankle was then attached with press-stud fastenings.

In this period the raw materials of elegance wools, silks, cottons, linings, buckles and buttons were becoming scarce. Even sewing thread became a problem. Europe and Italy were moving backwards: the silhouette was of course abandoned at this time of crisis and women's magazines (those few which survived) offered less stylized, streamlined ideals. Ration books and the cost of

foodstuffs on the black market took care of the extra pounds: no-one was overweight any more. Pattern-makers' imaginations ran in the opposite direction, with brains being wracked to ensure that women looked full

148. Wartime: for wear in the snow, knickerbockers type divided skirt in waterproof grey wool with high bodice and belt fastened with a buckle. The edges of the pockets are trimmed with red glass beads and red accessories are required. *Bellezza* 1942.

149. This feature was entitled "The Variety of Skirts" and emphasized the importance which Vanna, one of the most important designers, had given to the motifs on her skirts. Fulness taken to the back, draped, cross-over or fringed bands and detached, flowing panels manage to obtain excellent results for new kinds of elegance. *Bellezza* 1944.

148.

86.

of life, healthy and cheerful. Optimistic, cheeky little hats perched amongst hair puffed out by permanent waves. Shoulders were padded with wadds of cotton wool to give the figure more authority and a courageous air which a short skirt alone could not provide.

Skirts in poor quality cotton were swiftly provided with gathers to round thin hips.

In prolific Fascist Italy an exuberant body worthy of a goddess was still the ideal in 1940. In the meantime, in the United States and England women were called up to do military work. Attractive uniforms were created for nurses and women soldiers. Along the streets of London, skirts assumed a dry, sober look: below knee length, pockets inserted along the side seam and a gored cut in khakhi, or blue for women in the navy.

150. A cartwheel skirt with slash pockets and bib buttoned to wide shoulder straps is a casual, practical winter style. *Bellezza* 1942.

151. Idyllic pastoral skirt in cotton printed with stripes and flowers with an original belt/collar/strap motif. *Grazia* 1941.

149.

151.

All Europe's women, when they took off their working clothes, invented for themselves an exotic, holiday air, at a time when there was no point in talking about real holidays. They wore gathered skirts with large flowers and wore inexpensive cotton scarves, sometimes in the same pattern as their skirts, wrapped turban-style around their heads.

With all trade and travel not strictly related to the war interrupted, the fashion world was at a standstill. Changes in style were dictated by the need for self-sufficiency alone. Women walked on "orthopedic" shoes produced from bicycle tyres. The poor quality of the thin, flimsy fabrics produced from waste materials was concealed by showy prints. The designs of fabrics, in this period of bloodshed and violence, did not explore exotic lands and vegetation but dedicated themselves to the local countryside: idyllic meadows in bloom, poppies, cornflowers and ears of ripe corn tied in bunches alternated with bouquets of tulips with a more drawing-room air. Woodland flowers, violets, gentians and cyclamins were also present, while in Italy edelweiss was very much in fashion,

88

mainly to curry favour with the Germans.

Every country got to work to produce fabrics of all mineral or vegetable origins. In Italy viscose, derived from wood, flourished. People sang the praises of rayon, son of cellulose, which gleamed, if viewed from a respectful distance, exactly like silk.

THE CLAMOUR OF THE NEW LOOK

Once the war was over both women and skirts totally rejected uniforms and rediscovered the joy of flowing full cuts. The air was full of sensuality, the urge to dance, and *joie de vivre*. If at the end of 1947 the military-casual line was still dominant in fashion, the skirts of the neo-realist period were already beginning to feature drapes and a full, soft shape. The ambassadress for this image was Evita Perón, on a politics and promotion trip to Europe. She dressed like a vamp and her platinum gold hair glittered like a golden crown: she wore pin- stripe skirts with four pleats and very see-through nylon stockings.

When Christian Dior's New Look, which required circular long skirts reaching almost to the ankle, burst onto the scene, the general astonishment was soon overcome by the wish to dress with feminine enthusiasm.

Perhaps not everyone knows that the proportions proposed by the new style elegance had sound economic motives. It was Marcel Boussac, a French textile industrialist, who financed Dior and the New Look at the end of the war to use up or diversify his output of aviation cloths. The lengths required by this Paris fashion guaranteed immediate fabric consumption, which increased by twenty per cent worldwide.

The body was drawn in by *guêpières* and became terrifyingly sexy. The waistline was as slender as the torso, while the hips and bust were well rounded. Skirts reached down towards the ground, supported by a lining in *fliselina* or starched petticoats. In Dior's opinion, short skirts were lacking in

152. A checked wool skirt with straps crossed over at the back for the star of the film *Il birichino di papà. Bellezza* 1943.

153. An elegant tartan silk skirt portrayed by Henri Matisse, 1941.

153.

154. For the afternoon outfit Pierre Balmain designed a tight black skirt with an overlapping panel motif at the side and high shaped waistband. *Officiel* 1949.

155. On Wednesday, 12th February 1947 Christian Dior's "bombshell" exploded with the presentation of his spring-summer collection. The two lines, "Corolle" and "En huit", were then renamed "New Look" and presented long skirts just 30 cm from the floor.

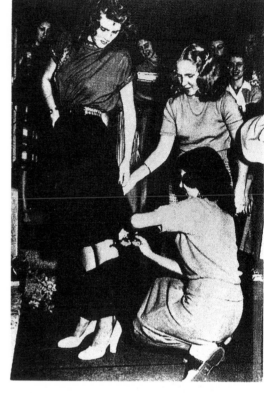

155.

156. Petticoat in contrasting fabric to decorate a straight princess dress for daytime wear. 1949.

154.

156.

157.158. The little straight or pleated skirts in patterned fabric, strictly reserved for beachwear, were the forerunners of the mini skirt. *Marie Claire* 1949.

all attraction, as were hotch-potches of colours and fabrics. The great French designer believed that all ensembles must be coordinated in unison, even to extremes: shoes, bag, gloves and skirt had to glow with the same colour shade, if possible dark or neutral.

The *jeunes filles en fleur* of the late Forties won a few concessions from their parents on the question of going out in the evenings and dressed accordingly. Beneath the rounded basque of a short jacket there appeared a satin cartwheel skirt in deep, dramatic colours: leaden grey, purple, copper and old gold. The intimate satisfaction of being dressed in the latest fashion, even if they all looked exactly the same, compensated these young ladies for the fatigue of long fitting sessions on their feet to allow the dressmaker, armed with ruler, chalk and pins, to mark the hemlines at the compulsory 30 cm from the floor (heel included).

159. A black faille overskirt emphasizes the flared line of the "bustier" dress. Dior, 1949.

THE ERA OF ITALIAN STYLE
THE FIFTIES

MORE CASUAL HABITS

In Europe, the lifestyle became healthy, simple, relaxed and noisy. Young people dressed, sat, danced and walked in imitation of the kids at U.S. colleges. Young girls wore low ballet-type shoes (*cenerentole* or "cinderellas") and nylon stockings whose transparency posed a problem to priests who did not allow bare legs in church. They floated on puffed out, full skirts cut in a full circle or in loose folds starting from the waist. The hemline was somewhere below the knee. Behaviour became more casual, to resemble that on the other side of the Atlantic, whence came formica kitchens, juke-boxes, and the geometrical beat of rock and roll. At meetings everyone sat on the ground and skirts popped up like so many multi-coloured flowers, even if no-one dared put their feet on the table which held the glasses of Coca-Cola, the thrilling substitute to the lemonades so dear to the Mediterranean middle classes.

These years saw the acceptance, without reserve, of those fabrics which have the astonishing power of not staining and of drying in a very short time without ironing. Even if the handle and hang were not perfect, round or dome-shaped skirts in tiny geometrical patterns were enthusiastically cut in the new fibres, which were completely man-made.

93

160. Girls dressed with practical ease. This loosely pleated skirt worn with a "turtle-neck" pullover was the classical outfit of the American college girl. *L'Officiel* 1950.

THE PORTENTS OF THE CONSUMER AGE

Wardrobes were becoming fuller, because in the consumer society clothes were less expensive. Young people were seduced by purchasing power, "to be, to want, to have", and "to be, to want, to change". The skirt became more widespread and had a profound influence at a symbolic level, since it allowed its owner to become, to transform, and to play on effects. Skirts were now worn at all hours of the day and also conquered the night time. For morning or holiday wear there were fluttering skirts in provençal taste.

Gala, Salvator Dalì's wife and muse, wore a Mediterranean skirt in "soleiado" fabric which looked like an assembly of

161.

162.

assorted coloured cotton scarves. She combined this with rope-soled shoes, a white linen blouse and a "casual" barbarian-style necklace in emeralds, ruby and gold.

The French ready-to-wear sector took hold of this unexplored folk theme and offered a wide range of peasant-style ideas at high prices. These were skirts with dense narrow stripes, held up by a sash-belt and gathered onto the waistband. The full final flounce was essential, with its stiffness ensured by the fact that the fabric was sewn double, or even quilted.

The United States, which had been cut off from messages from the Paris fashion world for five years during the Second World War, learnt to get by on their own and took a look at the folk history of their own continent. They created rustling Mexican skirts for sun outfits, with strapless bodices and "Baroque" bubble skirts featuring very gathered flounces decorated with wide strips of embroidered cotton laces.

161. A very full, fairly complex skirt with cuts and featured buttons. The fashion of the Fifties. *La Famìlia* 1952.

162.163.164. Skirts were almost indispensable for the beach, and matched the swimsuit or shorts and top. They could be embroidered, with contrasting trim, pleated or gathered as long as they were open, cross-over, fastened and with slits. *Annabella* 1956.

163.

164.

165.

166.

167.

168.

165.166.167. Stitching, slashed buttoned pockets, gathers and inserts. Everything goes provided the skirt is full and tight at the waist. *La Familia* 1952.

168. Cartwheel skirt in very bright printed cotton with a rather gypsified air: definitely summery in mood. *La Donna* 1951.

169. Embroidery was a very fashionable decorative motif in the Fifties, especially on summer skirts. The skirt decorated with bunches of tulips in satin stitch was by Emilia Bellini, an embroiderer from Florence. *Novità* 1952.

170.171. The early Fifties saw the opening of lots of boutiques selling imaginative clothes, especially in holiday centres. The skirts were in rustic cloth with embroidery, or in printed cottons, and shapes varied. *Novità* 1953, 1950.

169.

170.

171.

HIGH FASHION SKIRTS

The loser in this period, left to suffer alone in silent mortification, was the sober, casual skirt. People wanted to live and have fun, and for a fair number of seasons nobody was attracted by a simple line, so wrap-over skirts and kick-pleats disappeared. Everything which had anything to do with military severity was avoided like an unpleasant memory and moreover, as an alternative to such styles, ladies were acquiring the habit of wearing multi-coloured trousers, at least in a holiday setting. People were seized by a irresistible urge to assert their collective personality. Even dances had changed. Those slinking dances in couples were outmoded. Their place was taken by deafening, vaguely orgiastic beats which took possession of the dancers, who mimed erotic contorsions in public.

The skirt became seductive, very feminine, full, and provocative. It was held out by one or more petticoats or by a lining in the ever-present *fliselina*, a greyish

fabric as stiff as parchment which eliminated the "hard labour" of starching and gave "cartwheel" cuts an unexpected richness.

Haute couture, which observed all these happenings from afar, turned up its nose at the banal idea of the skirt as a separate garment in its own right, and would accept

98

172.

172. Bubble skirts were worn in the evening for elegant occasions. *Annabella* 1957.

173. Flowered cotton with bellows pockets, knotted cady panels giving an oriental effect, and fan-shaped pleats all round the figure fastened with knots. In silk surah. Models for everyday summer wear in town. *Annabella* 1956.

174. For evening wear, a flared skirt in gores with a very high bodice style waistband. *Bellezza* 1953.

173.

174.

175.

176.

it only as part of a suit. In Paris daytime creations used aristocratic pleated materials, and unrepeatable masterpieces of proportion emerged from the *ateliers* of Fath, Balmain and Dior. Suits had a short jacket with fitted waist, but their skirts could also be used with a cashmere sweater or twin-set, or a silk or linen shirt, provided the waistline was emphasised by a striking, broad, stiff belt.

The successions of pleats were sometimes interrupted by straight panels running down the hips: these offered undeniable advantages in terms of streamlining. Sunray pleats were available in thousands of variations.

It was only for the long, eye-catching evening skirt that haute couture, which had now taken on an Italian flavour, had an affectionate smile.

Puffed out with lots of silky semi-rigid

fabrics faille and various weights of taffeta alternated with bayadere twill full length or ankle-length for the younger woman, evening skirts were worn with fluttering blouses or bodices stiffened with whalebone and embroidery. The luxury of luxuries was the "two-piece" effect evening gown resembling a skirt and blouse created by Pierre Balmain, the French designer of the Jolie Madame line, which combined a long, black, severe, tight-fitting skirt with a white button-down blouse in snow-white ermine.

175.176. The brown flannel skirt in eight gores becomes striking when it is held out by the new crinoline which reappeared during these years: it was short, full, often with frills at the hem, in several layers of *fliselina* or nylon taffetta. *Vogue* 1951.

177. A panorama of skirts. To be in tone with the dictates of Paris haute couture skirts had to feature uneven drapes, be tight-fitting and slanting, and give a very slinky walk. *Vogue* 1950.

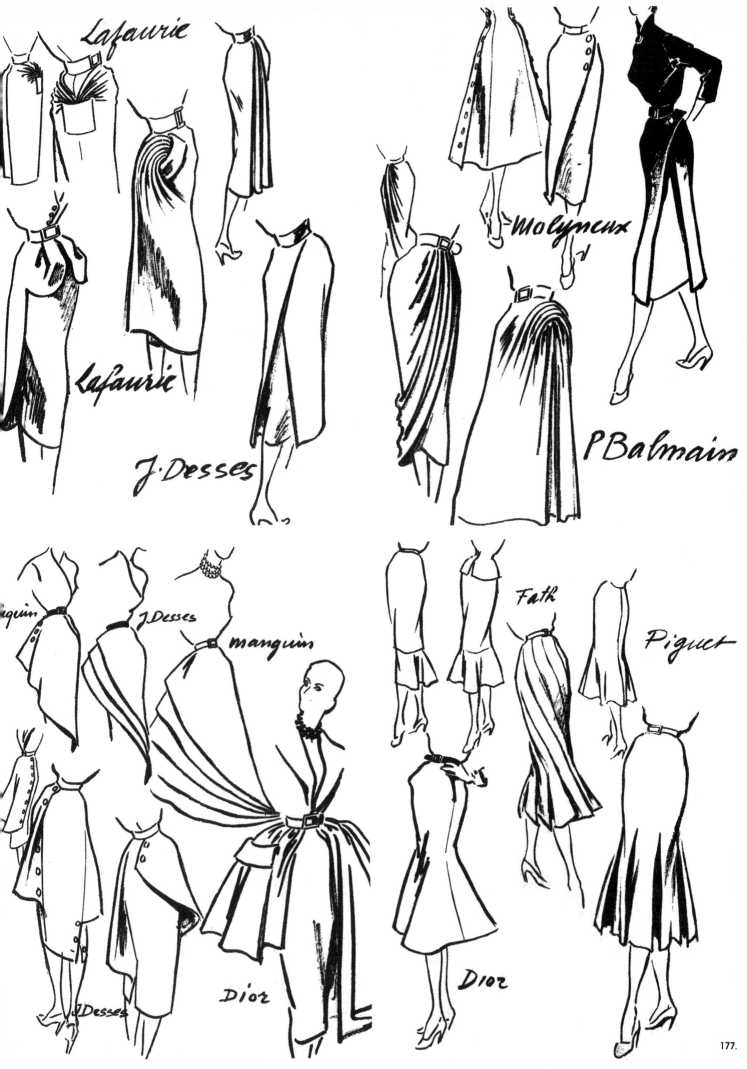

Lafaurie

Molyneux

Lafaurie

J. Desses

P Balmain

J. Desses

manguin

mauguin

Fath

Piguet

Dior

Dior

177.

GOSSIP ON KEY

In the Fifties, women lived through their sexiest moments of the century: the silver screens and the glossy magazines telling tales of the private lives of famous women were full of well-rounded figures. Cunning diagonal darts beside the bust and little loose pleats on the left and right of skirts added curves to curves. The myth of the "pin-up" or the well-endowed cover-girl was imposed as a new model of beauty, health and hope.

Gossip spread onto a wider dimension; leaving behind the balconies and courtyards where it had traditionally been exchanged, it left next-door neighbours in peace to concentrate on the celebrities of the world of printed paper.

Actresses and princesses alike showed off invitingly rounded shapes, underlined by guêpières and bubble skirts, in photographs which assumed more and more importance in relation to the texts

178. Pierre Balmain caught up all the fulness of this tartan skirt at the back. Cut on the bias, it was elegantly combined with a black velvet jacket. *L'Officiel* 1951.

179. The skirt of the spring suit is pleated with a high waistband fastened with three matching buttons. *L'Officiel* 1952.

178.

180.

180. This flannel skirt with unusual pleats giving a "spearhead" effect comes from an haute couture collection. *L'Officiel* 1952.

181. Schiaparelli, the greatest name in international haute couture, provided a tulle rainbow for an exceptional evening skirt. *Novità* 1952.

181.

which accompanied them. At the Pitti Palace in Florence, as Italian fashions were launched, designers also included skirts in their fashion parades for example the flared Venetian skirt pleated in both directions for a "lumpy" effect.

The wizard of the "made in Italy" skirt

179.

182.

183.

182.183. Made in Italy skirts by Franco Bertoli.

184. A "boutique" skirt in a hand-printed fabric by Falconetto, the Italian company where one of the most imaginative designers on the Italian ready-to-wear scene, Ken Scott, started his career. *Eva* 1957.

184.

was Bertoli. His creations were always in the same bell-shaped style, in thick hand-woven fabrics in the densest colours. Unfailingly decorated with braid edging, embroidered motifs in gold or silver and chenille figuring, they took up the regional folk styles, smuggling them into the world of ostentation and exporting the taste for Italian imagination.

For summer, a long skirt worn with a streamlined bodice gave way to meta-morphosis with folds taken in at the hem or lots of small pleats: these styles were in linen or shantung silk. Skirts in *mikado*, a stiff, translucid shot satin, in more garish colours, hung in a slight bell-shape, creating an appearance of stiffness always finishing in a bow on the high belt which was almost a bodice.

The long cotton skirts were often embroidered with coloured stones and sequins which emphasized the printed pattern by giving it glitter.

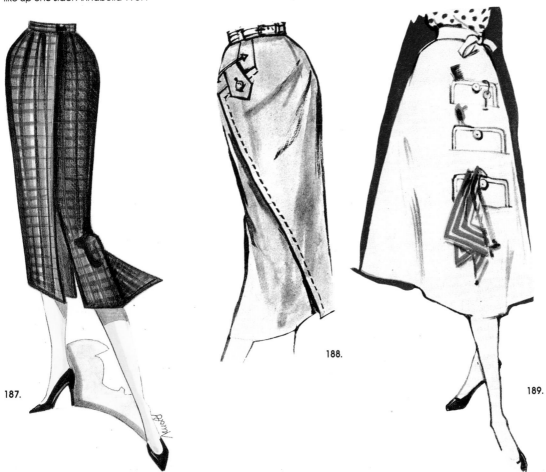

185. 186. Franco Bertoli, 1960s.

187. The casual divided skirt, in large-checked tweed, is enlivened by two loose panels.

188. Tight skirts always feature a sophisticated detail. In grey vicuna, this one uses stitching and a band formed by two fabric tabs. *Annabella* 1956.

189. A new idea for a summer skirt, white if possible, in linen, poplin or cotton gabardine. It is flared with pockets running step-like up one side. *Annabella* 1957.

185.

186.

187.

188.

189.

190. Full, lively and billowing, skirts were luxurious for evening too. Many were similar, decorated with braid, trimming, ribbons, and frothy edgings of pleated tulle which alternated on a coloured or dramatically black background. Designs by Bertoli, the "magician" of the made in Italy skirt, 1957-60.

MINI AND MAXI
THE SIXTIES

FIRST LADIES IN SKIRTS TOO

The disappearance of the generously sized pin-up girls coincided with the arrival of the pill. A few milligrams of oestregen rapidly revolutionalized the figure. Paradoxically, as soon as women felt themselves free from the threat of unwanted pregnancies, they showed that they had no wish to put themselves on show from a sexual point of view, with all their curves emphasized by carefully placed darts. The neurotic display of monster busts (a sign of repressed, frustrated sexuality) was no longer acceptable, and neither was the inviting flutter of full skirts, which now found themselves restricted to cocktail parties.

The liberated ladies and girls of the early Sixties chose their clothes to please themselves; not with seduction in mind but simply with the aim of feeling at ease.

The sociology of taste in the United States offered the masses a new image whose popularity lasted even though it was imitated at all levels. It was that of Jacqueline Kennedy, ex-journalist and now first lady. Her figure was completely different from those of the super-women

191. Very elegant tailored look skirt with a tunic effect with "barrel" line which Lancetti, the Roman designer, teamed up with a romantic black organza blouse. *La donna* 1963.

displayed on the pages of *Playboy*. Jacqueline, picking and choosing amongst the output of the world's designers, selected the best of the luxury ready-to-wear fashions. She loved bright pastel colours and no-fuss, dynamic skirts all line and details, emphasized by graphic stitching with discreet effects on the basque or interestingly shaped pockets. The hemline, just below the knee, did not hinder her nervy, edgy walk. Beneath the inevitable darts which gave roundness and softness to the hips the figure itself seemed almost masculine. The most popular skirts for morning wear finished in kick-pleats and were in herringbone tweed or tartan. The wrap-over skirts with braid edging were a homage to Coco Chanel.

For elegant afternoon occasions, shot taffeta and a full cut emphasized by loose pleats or suspended ribbing effects were *de rigueur*.

The important thing, if one wanted to be in fashion, was to take all drama out of the look by giving the blouse absolute priority: this had to be worn with the collar carelessly turned up and was accompanied by stiff trapezium-shaped skirts.

192.

192. At the beginning of the Sixties the skirts of suits had a very tailored look and were emphasized by the jackets, which were very short. Double stitching and stitched-edge box-pleat for reversible fabric. *Grazia* 1962.

193.-196. Even skirts created their own "style". Casual skirts were the basis of the wardrobe, according to a women's magazine in 1960. Skirts were everyday wear. Ideal for the office, shopping and travelling. All for wear with blouses, pullovers, tops and leather belts. *Grazia* 1960.

193.

194.

195.

196.

197.

198.199.

197. A traditional skirt from the Andes. It was to have considerable influence on taste and fashions in skirts in the years which followed. *Novella* 1961.

198.199. The "barrel" shaped skirt is slightly rounded towards the hemline. Hemlines now just covered the knee. *Novella* 1960. Summer skirts were almost always in cotton printed with cheerful, highly coloured, amusing floral designs. *Novella* 1961.

200.-203. Elegant skirts offered a large number of variations and were generally for younger women and girls. The "mikado" skirt has a large waistband instead of a belt. Hand-woven white wool with a woven border in pastel colours and golden braid. Bronze wool and lurex with irregular tucks and a stiff belt with bow and strass. Finally, a purple taffetta skirt with angled pleats creating a herringbone effect. *Grazia,* 1960.

200.

201.

202.

203.

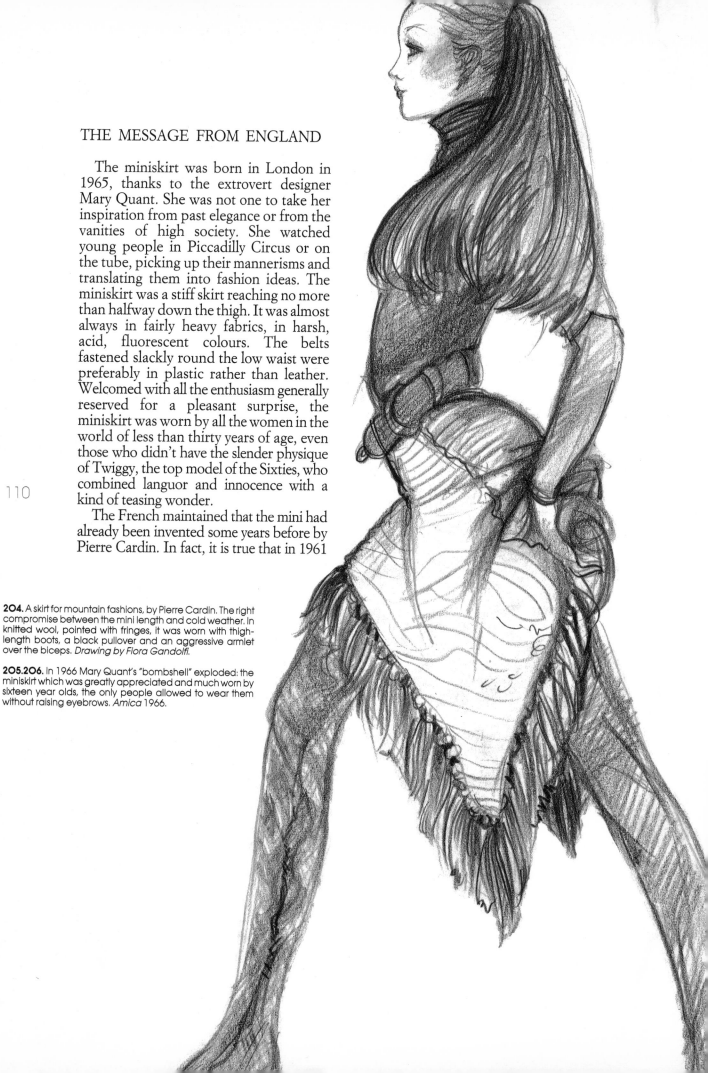

THE MESSAGE FROM ENGLAND

The miniskirt was born in London in 1965, thanks to the extrovert designer Mary Quant. She was not one to take her inspiration from past elegance or from the vanities of high society. She watched young people in Piccadilly Circus or on the tube, picking up their mannerisms and translating them into fashion ideas. The miniskirt was a stiff skirt reaching no more than halfway down the thigh. It was almost always in fairly heavy fabrics, in harsh, acid, fluorescent colours. The belts fastened slackly round the low waist were preferably in plastic rather than leather. Welcomed with all the enthusiasm generally reserved for a pleasant surprise, the miniskirt was worn by all the women in the world of less than thirty years of age, even those who didn't have the slender physique of Twiggy, the top model of the Sixties, who combined languor and innocence with a kind of teasing wonder.

The French maintained that the mini had already been invented some years before by Pierre Cardin. In fact, it is true that in 1961

110

204. A skirt for mountain fashions, by Pierre Cardin. The right compromise between the mini length and cold weather. In knitted wool, pointed with fringes, it was worn with thigh-length boots, a black pullover and an aggressive armlet over the biceps. *Drawing by Flora Gandolfi.*

205.206. In 1966 Mary Quant's "bombshell" exploded: the miniskirt which was greatly appreciated and much worn by sixteen year olds, the only people allowed to wear them without raising eyebrows. *Amica 1966.*

the French designer brought hemlines to a span above the knee, but he enclosed the legs in long stocking-boots in fabric or leather which were fastened to a suspender belt.

The sensational skirt of the day always had small side slits and patch or welt

205.

204.

206.

pockets. It was worn with socks or tights which could be sheer or in colours which matched the metallized enamel shoes.

In summer legs were bare, sun-tanned if possible, and a knitted vest top was required. The original English style was

207. Paco Rabanne started his attack on current fashions in France, using unusual materials for his clothes. Here, white leather strips feature for the "gladiator" style mini skirt held together by metal hooks. *Drawing by Flora Gandolfi.*

208. A mini-skirt in burnished chrome. Emanuel Ungaro, its creator, called it a "sculpture" for the body and stated that there was nothing more modern or more magical for a beautiful young woman. *Drawing by Flora Gandolfi.*

207.   208.

209. Mini-skirt in reversible wool heavy enough to ensure a stable hang. Chains were Chanel's idea for a casual, young style. *Annabelle* 1968.

209.

210.

diversified to offer mini-kilts, mini-wrap-over skirts, mini denim skirts and mini pleated skirts.

In 1969 the space age was well under way and skirts, which were already mini length, adopted a space-style linear cut. Printed patterns with references to flowers or leaves disappeared. The cold perfection of geometry, areas of colour outlined by lines and squares, metal accessories, and lunar and mineral images with silvery colours were all the rage.

210. The microskirt arrived from Paris to supplant the mini. Dior presented a huge bow and a handful of jewels (fake, of course) at the end of the longest of legs. *Drawing by Fiora Gandolfi* 1969.

The great designers transformed women into space travellers. The fabrics used were stiff and crush-resistant, often consisting of two layers glued together to eliminate crumples and linings completely.

There were a lot of reversible fabrics and compacted wools which hung like plastic tubes. The body was sealed into a container- dress. Skirt pockets took the shape of inspection hatches or television screens. Buttons, seen as medieval embellishments, disappeared, giving way to large, colourful zip fastenings which were a striking decorative feature.

Skirts in the lunar epoch were short and stiff, shuddering with horror at the very idea of a bow or a little drapery. The edges were emphasized by elegant turn-up stitching or padded trims. The intarsia pockets were round, oval or triangular, and harmonized with the haircut, in helmet shape. Everyday fashions, even if they cast a curious glance in the direction of Paco Rabanne's sheet metal skirts or Cardin's space-age bridal gown, preferred

the modern ascetism of Courrèges, a designer who imagined women as very busy, ascetically dressed town-dwellers. They wore white skirts and simplified blouson tops with lots of round-edged patch pockets in fresh pastel colours.

The dreamlike do-nothing world of the hippies provided a counterpoint to this hymn to energy and purity. The flower people were as happy as larks. Their skirts had nothing to do with the space age, cleanliness or the future: quite the opposite, they looked back to times past, the remote roots of Indo-European civilization, bright colours and weird mixtures, and the imperfection of hand-printed fabrics. Long and flared, gathered at the waist, in cotton or patchwork, they were a display of extroversion and

imagination which reflected the motto so dear to the revolutionary students of Paris: "power to the imagination." The same kind of long gipsy-style skirt was adopted as evening wear by the middle classes, who tried to reassure themselves against the tense revolutionary atmosphere of the period. These skirts were simple but luxurious, in leopard skin, when its use was not yet banned.

211. Italian fashions, more restrained, idealized a double petal-like mini-skirt with ribbing in a bright "Marlboro" red. *Drawing by Flora Gandolfi.*

212. A congress of space-age mini-skirts with portholes, low belts, man-made materials and an aggressive air. This was the style for Pierre Cardin's girls.

213. Ken Scott dressed women in ultra-modern style for summer evenings with femme fatale skirts in silk crepe with pleated panels and a drawstring low on the hips, combined with a bandeau and a fluttering scarf. A new oriental look, or a modernized view of Paul Poiret?

212.

213.

GIAGUARO

214. The Italian haute couture fur designer, Jole Veneziani, looked back to the fishtail line of the Thirties in a context of forbidden elegance: a long leopard-skin skirt.

THE LATEST SKIRTS

NEW MATERIALS FOR CREATIVE YEARS

The Seventies provided women who wished to achieve fuller knowledge of themselves by taking a clear view of their own personalities a pause for reflection. The geometry of the sexes, hitherto laid down in no uncertain terms by the male idea of things, had made differences imperative even where there was no reason for them. Now shapes were becoming less distinct and the unisex look, a kind of clothing for disguise, was born. Men wore brightly coloured pullovers, imaginative belts and white coats. They even stole women's handbags, which they converted into a more masculine version.

For their part, the members of the fair sex refused all clothing which emphasized melting curves or featured tight belts at the waist. They wore trousers with enthusiasm, but were also prepared to accept skirts which, in this period, were available in a wide variety of styles.

The world of skirts provided a faithful reflection of the fact that there were two

215. These shorts reaching to mid thigh were called "hot pants". They were worn with tight-fitting boots as long as stockings, and offered a break away from the much-discussed miniskirt. To reduce the shock, the fashion included an open overskirt of normal length. *Annabella* 1971.

opposing trends around: on the one hand was the wish to maintain the economic gains made in the previous years, while the other side of the coin was a sincere interest in radical moral and political changes. One example of this antithesis was the display of skirts in all sizes, mini, maxi or midi, in luxury furs such as broadtail, mink, ocelot, zebra, monkey and jaguar. This was the period of the first skirts in chamois leather or light suede, materials never previously used for this purpose, which invaded the world's fashion markets thanks to Italian skill and inventiveness.

216. The "cave-woman" leather skirt gave its wearer an aggressive, wild, free look.

217. A luxury pretend guerilla. A cartridge belt, a Western-style hat and the simple cut with large front pleat give a less formal air to the sophisticated, luxurious mink skirt. *Annabella* 1970.

216.

218.

UNUSUAL MATERIALS
FOR NEW SIZES

In these years of self-rediscovery women, who thought, spoke and chose for themselves, realized that there was not just one type of beauty. The cinema itself continually offered and overlapped different kinds of grace and style. Barbra Streisand's talent and character led viewers to forget the unevenness of her face. Vanessa Redgrave, thin as an X-ray picture, was stunning.

218. Four layers of muslin in different patterns and colours make up an original skirt of gypsy inspiration. It looks back to the hippy style which the student protests of the previous years had brought into fashion. *Amica* 1970.

219. A pop art mini-skirt sticks its tongue out. *Grazia* 1971.

219.

Monica Vitti transformed a husky voice into a sexy attribute and a pronounced nose into a hallmark of personal attraction.

Each of these women "fulfilled" herself and dressed in her own style. The first step was to reject the dress, because it was too conventional in appearance and did not allow for invention and variations on themes. Skirts, with their capacity for "lucid" transformations were more fun, allowing free associations of extrovert, unusual outfits.

Women changed their images to fit their moods and their whims, and there were no longer different styles of dressing for different times of day.

At the seaside at Positano in the 1970 season skirts were gipsy, peasant or oriental style. The indispensable accessories were flat open sandals and rustic jewellery in wood, string and leather.

The skirt for leisure wear, if it wanted a countrified effect, involved a short skirt worn over a longer one in seersucker pattern. The three-flounced skirt for wear over clogs featured frills trimmed with multi-coloured ribbons. At the cinema everyone was now on the Red Indians' side against the "heroes", who continued to turn up, upsetting years of culture and commonplaces.

The skirt became an item of clothing which reflected all the new populist ideas and continually reworked ideas from the most distant cultures: Indian, African, Mexican and so on. These were not copies as such, because the shapes were taken to extremes or toned down by the use of luxury materials unusual in this setting. Folk style skirts had fun with gauze, flannel, and cottons, but gave off a special and very different perfume when they

were in cashmere, vicuna or silk.

The fringe was typical of the fashions derived from Apache or Comanche folklore, as were insets of little pearls, lace fastenings, and hemlines hacked away with scissors to imitate primitive skirts sewn with bone needles.

220. At the beginning of the Seventies everything may have seemed normal at first glance but skirts featured astonishing slits for surprising effects. *Grazia* 1971.

221. An elegant pleated mini-skirt for spring wear in silk crepe worn casually under a blue cloth jacket. *Jours de France* 1972.

222. After the mini had come and gone, skirts remained decidedly shorter. They stopped just above the knee. The overlapped white wool skirt fastened with a huge safety pin is a faithful reproduction of the Scottish kilt. *Jours de France* 1972.

221

222.

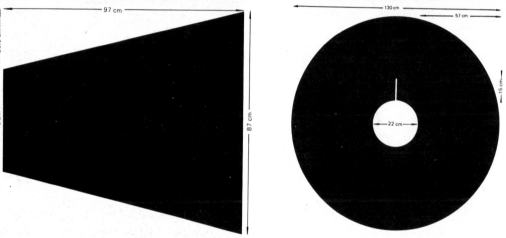

223. A perfect circle, a circular hole 22 cm in diameter in the centre and.. voilà, a cartwheel skirt in canvas, cotton or flannel, as long as it was a total-width fabric. Two trapezia cut on the bias, two seams and a drawstring, and a long skirt for summer social occasions was ready. *Marie Claire* 1972.

224. The "rag" skirt, an episode which was parallel to and not connected to the "women's lib" period of the Seventies. Feminism was on the up, and witches were back, spreading the "Ad lib" fashion which expressed opposition to conventional morality and the demand for sexual freedom through uneven hemlines. 1975.

225. A design whim using the skirts which were part of India's ancient culture. Different finenesses of cotton and silk thread were woven on a hand loom. Missoni. Photo by William Connors, *Vogue* 1974.

224.

225.

226.   227.   228.

226.229. The right reaction against ultra-short skirts was to offer a very long skirt for daytime wear, in a length which just revealed the ankle. Here it is in heavy wool gores, "English secretary" style in tweed, more sophisticated in pale cashmere and more romantic in grey velvet with white lace frills. Photos by Carlo Orsi, *Vogue* 1973.

230. A new mania "antique fashions", appeared on the scene. Full skirts full of flounces, embroidery and cotton lace, taken from old trunks in the attic or from the memory of grandmothers and great-grandmothers. They were simple and often white, but sometimes appeared highly coloured, resembling the starched petticoats of crinolines and skirts taken from the Mexican, Creole and gypsy traditions. *100 Idées* 1975.

AGGRESSIVE AND DISTURBING TO SUIT ALL TASTES

The line of the knitted skirts offered in the Sala Bianca (White Saloon) of the Pitti Palace in Florence gave a message of more sophisticated elegance, without reducing the comfort level: tight waists and figure-restricting shapes were definitely out. The silhouettes shown in the fashion magazines were long and soft.

Knits, jersey, and tricot with tiny multi-coloured jacquard designs or with tiny, repetitive geometrical motifs were used to produce an unforgettable series of skirts emphasizing a clothing style which neither suppressed nor exaggerated the female figure. Women, who had become their own bosses, no longer had any need to show off their hidden shapes.

For evening wear, the skirt and top in different fabrics were in fashion. The skirts were long and trapezium-shaped, with a high slit at the front, worn with dizzingly high platform shoes and lamé or satin blouses which were always inspired by military styles.

In 1971 the first hot-pants, with highly revealing length and fit, were presented at fashion shows beneath classical, masculine-cut jackets. Naturally they were not acceptable to all women, and many accepted the compromise of covering them with a skirt open to the waist.

The final items in the fashion parades were safari and guerilla skirts, which offered lots of bellows pockets and cartridge belts worn low on the hips for "dangerous" terrain.

They were in camouflage colours and used military-style fabrics.

The strongly reformist mood of the times, with Monsignor Lefebvre's rebellion in favour of the Latin mass, President Nixon's resignation over Watergate and the energy crisis, changed the outlines of the political and social status quo. Trends became more extreme and the pop fashion for "intentional ugliness" was born.

The pale blue hats of suffocating Anglo-Saxon middle-class morality were shocked

231. One of the queens of the French prêt-à-porter world, Sonia Rykiel, offered a very attractive midi (mid-calf) length skirt in ecru cotton crepe printed with black and dark flowers in classical cretonne pattern for town wear in summer. *Marie France* 1974.

229.

230.

231.

126

232.

233.

by satin mini skirts which offended the sensibilities with impossible colour combinations. At the same time the nude look came down from the bodice to the skirt, which became transparent, partially see-through or slashed by incredible openings.

232. The skirt attracted the attention of Italy's fashion "greats" not only for use in suits but also as a separate item. Biki created a skirt in heavy silk cady with pleats and a dazzling split at the hip. 1978.

233. Chanel presented an "old-fashioned" look in 1978. Beneath a classical jacket with lots of pockets and gold buttons was a straight wrap-over skirt with the hemline below the knee in wide-weave wool fabric, tripped with a woollen braid. *Hogar y Moda* 1978.

234. Valentino offered a fairy tale air with romantic post-modern skirts which, between flounces, were perhaps rather surprised to find themselves in his stylized gardens. 1978.

235. To give a carefree, fluttering walk, Ferré inserted a panel of pressed pleats on the hip of a grey flannel skirt. *Drawing by Fiora Gandolfi* from *Femina Lausanne* 1979.

127

234.

235.

236. For the leap into the next decade, a "bunch" of multicolour organzas held up by an elastic waistband and a belt. From the Italian ready-to-wear sector.

237. The starlet skirt in soft suede with silver lamé effect. Model by Gherardini.

238. Inspired by the folklore of Samarkand, Lancetti presented a skirt with gathered flounces in bright colours. 1980.

236.

TOWARDS THE END WE'RE BACK AT THE BEGINNING

The whirlwind of every possible extravagance finally came to rest, ironically enough, on the straight, tight, black starlet style tube skirt which reminded everyone that women had curves and, if they wanted to, could show them off.

The starlet style was offered as an optional alternative to the other way of dressing which springs to mind as typical of the late Seventies, which was based on the appealingly awkward, uncertain male style garments worn by Diane Keaton in Woody Allen's films.

During these years the concept of beauty recovered some of its sensuality. Roles came back into fashion to a certain extent, and with them the principles of elegance divided into clearly defined

237.

238.

compartments: morning, afternoon and evening not as rigidly divided as in the past, but with definite borderlines.

The suit for daytime wear, with a jacket of classical cut sporting bellows pockets, was worn with a beige wool skirt with three semi-sewn pleats on the front, or with an ivory coloured skirt with side slits.

The dry, clearly structured skirt gave way, for evening, to organza and a bunch of overlapped skirts in parrot colours, held up at the waist by a broad band of shiny leather.

Black evening suits, which served the same purpose as the male dinner jacket with its silken lapels, were on their way back. The skirt was tight-fitting and the inevitable slit was emphasized by a trim in the same colour as the lapel.

For evening wear, the winning ensemble was still the pleated voile skirt

240.

239.

241.

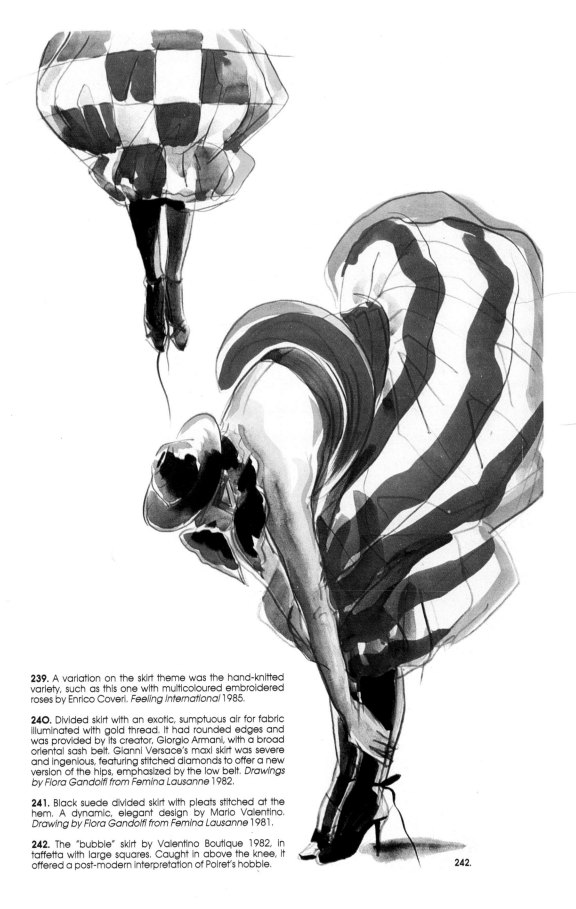

239. A variation on the skirt theme was the hand-knitted variety, such as this one with multicoloured embroidered roses by Enrico Coveri. *Feeling International* 1985.

240. Divided skirt with an exotic, sumptuous air for fabric illuminated with gold thread. It had rounded edges and was provided by its creator, Giorgio Armani, with a broad oriental sash belt. Gianni Versace's maxi skirt was severe and ingenious, featuring stitched diamonds to offer a new version of the hips, emphasized by the low belt. *Drawings by Fiora Gandolfi from Femina Lausanne* 1982.

241. Black suede divided skirt with pleats stitched at the hem. A dynamic, elegant design by Mario Valentino. *Drawing by Fiora Gandolfi from Femina Lausanne* 1981.

242. The "bubble" skirt by Valentino Boutique 1982, in taffetta with large squares. Caught in above the knee, it offered a post-modern interpretation of Poiret's hobble.

242.

which opened out like a theatre curtain to reveal a pair of equally pleated Bermuda shorts. There were also unsymmetrical touches which indicated the desire for change, with wrap-over skirts which opened out like petals or diagonally, or even displayed a zig-zag edge.

A dress or skirt had to reveal social and financial standing. The wish to display wealth and power returned to the forefront with expensive skirts in suede or multicoloured leathers interwoven by hand, or tight-fitting designs in ostrich, python or even eel skin.

243.244.245. Restless fashions, looking for a carefree image, casuals tended to acquire chic by the addition of a big name from the ready-to-wear world who designed creations in denim.

It seemed that the road towards real or presumed functionality had come to a dead end. Women who wanted to, and who had a suitably highly developed sense of humour, rushed to reinterpret Fifties styles by wearing skirts with unexpected coloured bows on the behind.

246.247. A young prestigious name in the French fashion world, Jean-Paul Gaultier experimented with new clothing formulae. The old gold satin skirt appeared with a motor-cyclist's jacket. Photo by Graziano Ferrari, *Allure* 1986. Another idea was a white linen skirt appearing beneath the cross-over, twisted hemline of a striped pareo-dress for an unusual, very amusing total look. *Elle* 1986.

133.

ON THE WAY TO THE YEAR 2000

The everyday skirt was now put into second place, serving as a background for a sparkling top which revealed batwing sleeves or luminous embroidery when the wearer raised her arms.

The top became even more important when years ago now the Italian television announcers started appearing from the waist upwards, leaving their lower halves to the viewers' imagination. Skirts or trousers? This was the question.

The skirt, since this is the item which interests us, rose and fell depending on the mood of the moment. Mini-dresses were worn with coloured knitted tights, or skirts with dramatic slits teamed with black stockings featuring eye-catching designs.

The shapeless Japanese style skirts with a drawstring waist were in crumpled cloth. Jean-Paul Gaultier, drawing on an absolutely new language, revitalized the classical items from Grandmother's trunk: a white

248.

cotton lacy petticoat was worn over a striped silk skirt. The factors were inverted but the attractiveness of the result was unchanged.

The "lampshade" skirt tucked up the hem and brought Poiret's *entrave* back into fashion, placing it at the bottom of the skirt where it was decorated with sculpted

248. The tight-fitting draped flannel skirt is from the Italian ready-to-wear scene. Gianmarco Venturi 1987.

249. When it comes to skirts Ferré, the fashion architect, has a lot to say. Sexy, aggressive cotton crepe skirt with a broad knitted band. Photo by Graziano Ferrari, *Allure* 1986.

250. Italian designers opted for the miniskirt: Gianni Versace's suit uses one with draped flounces.

251. Kenzo skirt in a filmy, loosely hanging fabric is wrap-over design with peplum-style drapes. 1987.

249.

250.

251.

252.253. Rich, elegant, sinuous, lively, fun-loving Carmen-style evening skirts bring all the fashion parades to a close, leaving every chance of a dancing entry to the new century. Models by Fausto Sarli and Valentino.

254. Capucci provides a short knee-length skirt worn with a black cloth jacket with unexpected three-dimensional waves of folded satin. Photo by Rudy Faccin von Steidl, *Collezioni* n. 2, 1987.

252.

253.

255. A double pleated frill emerges at hip-height from a basque made of horizontally gathered fabric. The effect is that of an upside down campanula. The designer: Valentino Garavani for the 1987 haute couture collections. Photo Rudy Faccin von Steidl, *Collezioni* n. 2, 1987.

255.

254.

draperies formed like a high-relief.

All the items in the wardrobe had to submit to the prevarications of transformism. Mini, knee or calf length, without restricting the stride of its wearer, the skirt was a continuous reminder that fashion is always running through fashions, so the road to the year 2000 seems to be paved with skirts inspired by large ambitious projects.

Although they have become ductile enough to allow an exchange of ideas between their creators and their wearers, skirt fashions will certainly continue to feature new details and new inventions which will date the garments beyond doubt, distinguishing them clearly from all previous styles.

256. Evening skirt in chiffon by Giorgio Armani. 1987

APPENDIX

GLOSSAR

ITALIANO	ENGLISH	FRANÇAIS	DEUTSCH
Baschina	**Basque**	Empiècement	Schösschen
Bretelle	**Braces**	Bretelles	Träger
Cintura	**Belt**	Ceinture	Gürtel
Drappeggio	**Draping**	Drapé	Drapierung
Fusciacca	**Sash**	Ceinture drapée	Schärpe
Girovita	**Waist**	Tour de taille	Taille
Gonna	**Skirt**	Jupe	Rock
abbottonata	**Button-through skirt**	boutonnée	Durchgeknöpfter Rock
diritta	**Straight skirt**	droite	Gerader Rock
sbieca	**Bell skirt**	en biais	Glockenrock
a quattro teli	**Gored skirt**	à quatre pans	Bahnenrock
a balze	**Flounce skirt**	volantée	Stufenrock
a pieghe, vita lunga	**Corso skirt**	à empiecèment	Sattelrock mit Falten
a ruota	**Wheel skirt**	cloche	Tellerrock
arricciata	**Gathered skirt**	froncée	Angekrauster Rock
pantaloni	**Pantskirt**	pantalon	Hosenrock
portafoglio	**Wrapover skirt**	portefeuille	Wickelrock
sportiva	**Sports skirt**	sportive	Sportlicher Rock
svasata	**Flaring skirt**	evasée	Aussgestellter Rock
in pelle	**Leather skirt**	en cuir	Lederrock
Impuntura	**Stitching**	Surpiqûre	Steppnaht
Minigonna	**Miniskirt**	Minijupe	Minirock
Nervature	**Ribs**	Nervures	Rippen
Orlo	**Hem**	Ourlet	Saum
Pettorina	**Bib**	Bavette	Latz
Pieghe	**Pleats**	Plis	Falten
fermate	**Tucks**	cousus	Abgenähte Falten
baciate	**Inverted pleats**	creux	Kellerfalten
Piegoni	**Box pleats**	grand plis	Quetschfalten
Pieghettato	**Pleating**	Plissé	Plissiert
Sbieco	**Cross; bias**	Godet	Schrägbahn
Sottogonna	**Petticoat**	Jupon	Unterrock
Tasca	**Pocket**	Poche	Tasche
applicata	**Patch pocket**	appliquée	Aufgesetzte Tasche
a filetto	**Slant welt pocket**	fendue	Einggesetzte Tasche
a soffietto	**Bush flap pocket**	saharienne	Saharienne Tasche
con pattina	**Flap pocket**	avec revers	Tasche mit Klappe

ESPAÑOL	РУССКИЙ	注	释
Faldón	Баска	フラップ	緊身上衣
Tirantes	Бретели	サスペンダー	肩帯
Cinturón	Пояс	ベルト	腰帯
Drapeado	Драпировка	ドレープ	褶子
Fajín	Перевязь	サッシュ	宽饰帯
Cintura	Край юбки	ウエスト	腰身
Falda	Юбка	スカート	裙子
abotonada	застегнутая	ボタンつきスカート	帯钮扣的裙子
recta	прямая	スリムスカート	直裙
sesgada	косая	バイアススカート	斜裙
de cuatro paños	в четыре ширины	四枚はぎスカート	四幅做成的裙子
de volantes	с воланами	フラウンスドスカート	荷叶边的裙子
de canesù	с оборками	ロングウエストプリーツスカート	长腰,褶裙
acampanada	со складками	サーキュラースカート	张开裙
fruncida	в виде колокола	ギャザースカート	百褶裙
pantalón	с завивками	キューロットスカート	裙裤
carpeta	панталоны	巻スカート	褶送裙
deportiva	в виде портфеля	スポーツスカート	运动式裙
de linea trapecio	спортивная	フレアースカート	三角裙
de piel	раструбная	レザースカート	皮裙
	из кожи		
Pespuntes	Строчка	ステッチ	密缝
Minifalda	Миниюбка	ミニ	超短裙
Alforzillas	Нервюры	リブ	凸条
Dobladillo	Подол	すそ	折边
Peto	Вставка	ビブ	无袖胸衣
Pliegues	Складки	プリーツ	褶痕
cosidos	– закрепленные	タック	缝制褶痕
bésame	– соприкасающиеся	インバーテッドプリーツ	对称褶痕
Tablas	Большие складки	ボックスプリーツ	大褶痕
Plisado	Плиссированный	プリーツの入った	衣褶
Godé	Косой	バイアス	斜裁
Enagua	Нижняя юбка	ペティコート	衬裙
			口袋
Bolsillo	Карман	ポケット	贴袋
de plastrón	– накладной	パッチポケット	内袋
a ojal	– прорезной	スラントポケット	折送袋
de fuelle	– в гармошку,	アコーデオンポケット	盖袋
de tapeta	– с клапаном	フラップポケット	

BIBLIOGRAPHY

BOOKS

1830 - G. Ferrario, *Il costume antico e moderno di tutti i popoli*, Vincenzo Batelli, Firenze.

1930 - A. Panzini, *La penultima moda*, Paolo Cremonese, Roma.

1933 - A. Martini, *Moda 1790 - 1900*, Rizzoli & C., Milano.

1947 - M. von Böhn, *La moda*, Salvat, Barcelona.

1948 - A. Lejard, *Matisse*, Hazan, Paris.

1950 - R. Klein, *Lexicon der Mode*, Baden-Baden.

1951 - M. Leloir, *Dictionnaire du Costume*, Paris.

1955 - C. Beaton, *Lo specchio della moda*, Garzanti, Milano.

1962 - M. Garland, *Fashion*, New York.

1965 - U. Eco, *Apocalittici e integrati*, Bompiani, Milano.

1965 - *Encyclopaedia Britannica*, 15th edition William Benton.

1966 - *Cronica del siglo XX*, Plaza & Janes, Barcelona.

1966 - *Storia Universale dell'Arte: Arte Egizia; Dai Sumeri ai Cristiani; Il Settecento in Italia*, Fabbri, Milano.

1967 - S. Tchudi Madsen, *Fortuna dell'Art Nouveau*, Il Saggiatore, Milano.

1968 - Bofill y otros, *La mujer en Espana*, Cultura Popular, Barcelona.

1968 - G. d'Assailly, *Les 15 révolutions de la mode*, Hachette, Paris.

1969 - C. Ravaioli, *La donna contro se stessa*, Laterza, Bari.

1969 - E. Sullerot, *La donna e il lavoro*, Etas Kompass, Verona.

1975 - A.P. Céchov, *Racconti*, Einaudi, Torino.

1977 - *Guida alla Biblioteca di Palazzo Grassi*, Centro Arti e Costume, Milano.

1978 - T. Tierney, *Gibson Girls*, Dover Publications, New York.

1978 - T. Tierney, *Glamorous Movie Stars of the Thirties*, Dover Publications, New York.

1979 - G. Corsi, *L'Italia dal barbiere*, Bestetti, Milano.

1981 - M. Andronicos, *Musée d'Heracleion*, Ekdotike Athenon, Athenai.

1981 - G. Piersanti a cura di, *I grandi magazzini*, Savelli, Milano.

1982 - F. Ricci e E. Pifferi, *Lario fine secolo - Immagini di un viaggio*, E.P.I. Como.

1982 - Young S., *Betty Bonnet Paper Dolls*, Dover Publications, New York.

1983 - U. Pericoli, *Le divise del duce*, Rizzoli, Milano.

1984 - M. Jubb, *Cocoa & Corsets*, Idea Books, London.

1984 - A. Volker, *Wiener mode + Modefotografie*, Schneider-Henn, München, Paris.

1984 - S. Sabarsky, *Egon Schiele*, Mazzotta, Milano.

1985 - *Tessuti Costumi e Moda (raccolte storiche di palazzo Mocenigo)*, La Stamperia di Venezia, Venezia.

1985 - *Weekend Guide, La Grecia*, Istituto Arti Grafiche, Bergamo.

1986 - A. Piazzi e K. Lagerfeld, *Anna Chronique*, Longanesi, Milano.

1986 - *Futurismo e futurismi*, Catalogo, Bompiani, Milano.

1986 - *Paul Poiret et Nicole Groult* Catalogo Musée du Palais Galliera, Paris.

s.d. - M. Beaulieu, *Le costume moderne*, Presse Universitaire de France, Paris.

s.d. - W. Bruhn & M. Tilke, *L'abbigliamento nei secoli*, Edizioni Mediterranee, Roma.

s.d. - P.L. de Giafferri, *L'historie du costume feminin français*, Nilsson, Paris.

s.d. - P.L. de Giafferri, *L'histoire du costume feminin mondial*, Nilsson, Paris.

s.d. - M. Tilke, *Fogge di costumi e di vestiario*, Edizioni Mediterranee, Roma.

MAGAZINES

1866 - 1868: *La mode illustrée*

1900: *La saison*

1900 - 1909; 1915: *La mode illustrée*

1904: *La Domenica del Corriere*

1906; 1911; 1913; 1924: *La mode pratique*

1907: *Les modes*

1909; 1912; 1920 - 1921; 1928 - 1932: *Femina*

1912 - 1914: *Journal des dames et des modes*

1917 - 1919: *Pictorial review*

1926; 1950 - 1951: *Vogue*

1930 - 1940: *Le jardin des modes*

1932 - 1934: *Lidel*

1936 - 1939: *Dea*

1939 - 1941: *Grazia*

1942 - 1944: *Bellezza*

1944: *Fili moda*

1946: *Bellezza*

1949: *Marie Claire*

1949: *Le jardin des modes*

1949 - 1952: *L'Officiel*

1951; 1963: *La donna*

1951 - 1952; *Eva*

1952 - 1957: *Annabella*

1952: *Collections*

1952: *La famìlia*

1952 - 1964: *Novità*

1953: *Bellezza*

1957 - 1958: *Bellezza*

1960 - 1961: *Novella*

1960 - 1962: *Annabella*

1966: *Amica*

1967 - 1969: *Vogue Italia*

1970: *Elle*

1970 - 1971: *Annabelle*

1970: *Amica*

1971: *Grazia*

1972: *Jours de France*

1978 - 1982: *El Hogar y la Moda*

1979: *Annabella*

1979: *Vogue Italia*

1980 - 1981: *Femina* Lausanne

1985: *Feeling International*

1986: *Allure*

1986: *Elle*

1987: *La Gazzetta dello Sport*, 11 Aprile

1987: *Collezioni Alta Moda*

1987: *Collezioni P.A.P.*

Printed in October 1989 by Sagdos S.p.A. - Brugherio (MI)
Paper: CTS - Cartiera del Timavo e del Sole S.p.A. - Assago (MI)

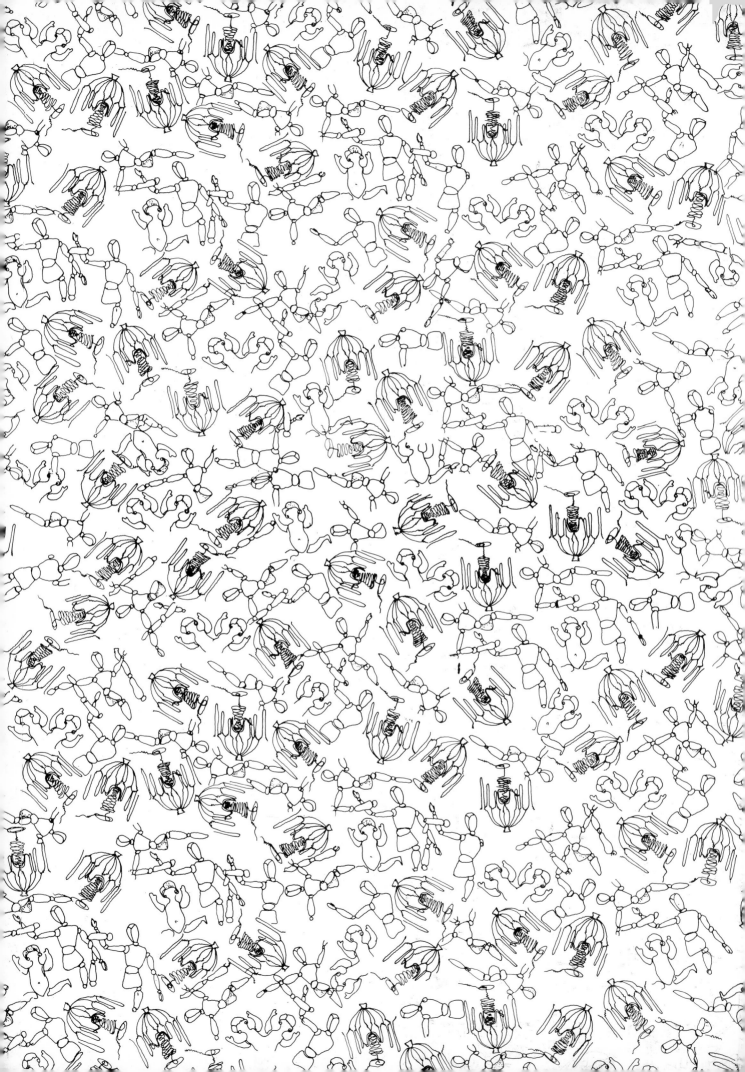